# teach with style

## Creative Tactics for Adult Learning

### Updated and Enhanced

Jim Teeters &
Lynn Hodges

ASTD
PRESS

**ASTD Press** is an internationally renowned source of insightful and practical information on workplace learning, performance, and professional development.

ASTD Press
1640 King Street Box 1443
Alexandria, VA 22313-1443 USA

**Ordering information:** Books published by ASTD Press can be purchased by visiting ASTD's website at store.astd.org or by calling 800.628.2783 or 703.683.8100.

Library of Congress Control Number: 2013937452
ISBN-10: 1-56286-856-X
ISBN-13: 978-1-56286-856-7
e-ISBN: 978-1-60728-549-6

**ASTD Press Editorial Staff:**
Director: Glenn Saltzman
Manager, ASTD Press: Ashley McDonald
Community of Practice Manager, Learning & Development: Juana Llorens
Associate Editor: Stephanie Castellano
Text and Cover Design: Marisa Kelly

Printed by Versa Press, Inc., East Peoria, IL, versapress.com.

# Contents

# Preface

The concept of *Teach With Style* was first put into print in 1997, in a self-published version by Jim Teeters. The second version, also by Jim, was published by Redleaf Press in 2001 and was primarily geared toward trainers of childcare providers. Now we offer this third version to be used by anyone who teaches adults in any setting or field.

This current version draws on our combined experience in teaching adults—more than 70 years' worth! Jim's experience includes training volunteers, family-life education, college teaching, government training management, religious education, and private consultation and training. Lynn started her path in adult education while on special assignment with her airline job, teaching flight attendants service skills, safety and first aid, leadership and conflict management, and post-9/11 security. She is currently an independent contractor coaching and teaching presentation skills, and has returned to the airline industry as a flight attendant, where she enjoys traveling and volunteering for special assignments that involve her training skills.

What is unique about *Teach With Style*? We present a dynamic model built around four unique instructor styles, each of which includes strategies for effective training. In addition, you'll find more than 120 learning activities, sample workshops, and other tools to help you continually improve as an instructor.

We invite you to dive in and learn. Our model has lots to offer to both new and experienced educators and trainers. We believe that if you put this information to use in your classroom, you are guaranteed to become an effective teacher of adults.

# Introduction

*We wish to dedicate this book to all the adult participants in our classes and workshops who have taught us about learning and helped us to develop the Teach With Style model!*

Experienced or new, adult instructors can be rigid in their approach to teaching. Usually we keep abreast of our particular topic of interest and expertise, but we may stagnate in the *way* we teach it. What keeps us growing, changing, and progressing? We need to see ourselves accurately through the eyes of our participants and colleagues, and we need a clear method to examine and improve our practice.

The concepts and tools in *Teach With Style* are designed to help you teach better no matter what the setting or how experienced you are. This model applies to any teaching situation, whether it's a seminar, a college course, an employee training session, or new-employee coaching. The model includes four simple instructor styles with strategies and learning activities to help you teach effectively—that is, your adult learners will learn and apply what you teach.

You will find *Teach With Style* the perfect guide for continuing improvement. Conscientiously followed, this simple program ensures positive results using an approach your adult learners will truly enjoy.

## Child and Adult Learners

One drizzly Sunday afternoon in Seattle, while Jim sipped coffee and gazed out a bakery window, a young mother suddenly zipped past, pushing her toddler in a stroller. With wide sparkling eyes the child greeted this common, everyday street scene as if it were a garden of delights. He seemed to be shouting, "Show me everything—I want it all!" If all adult learners came to our workshops and classes with that same attitude, how easy it would be to teach! Yet how differently adults and children approach learning.

Young children approach learning with a singularity of focus. They want to absorb all that they are shown and taught. When you teach something to young children, you do not need to prove to them that it's worth their while to learn it. They assume that it is.

It is our experience that most adult learners have quite a different attitude toward being taught. When adult learners say "Show me!" they are often admonishing the instructor to make the learning really count for something. Adults hope their time is well spent, because time spent on learning competes with the more immediate demands of life.

The unspoken demands of busy adult learners are:

- Show me why I should learn what you want to teach me.
- Show me that you are knowledgeable about this topic and worthy of my time and attention.
- Show me that you can hold my interest.
- Show me that you care enough to teach me what I want and need to learn.

Instructors are challenged to make their instruction meet the real needs of adult learners, and to clearly demonstrate the benefits of committing time to a seminar, class, or conference.

## Complexity of Adult Learners

One might think adults should be easy to teach because they are responsible and well behaved. On the contrary, we have found that adults present a formidable challenge to instructors. Adults add greater complexity to the classroom than young children do, because they (consciously or unconsciously) evaluate you (the instructor) and the learning experience while they are engaged in learning. This demands a deeper level of self-awareness from the adult instructor. You must constantly evaluate how you teach, what you teach, and how adult learners receive it.

Adults' expectations of the learning experience contribute to this complexity. As soon as adults hear about your workshop or class, they begin to develop expectations about it. They anticipate it with varying degrees of skepticism or interest, influenced by their past learning experiences. While they learn, adults also evaluate you and whether their expectations for the class are being met. This ongoing evaluation by learners can grossly or subtly affect how much they learn.

Adults have lived longer than children and therefore bring a multifaceted range of human emotions and personal histories to the learning place. They have learned to mask strong feelings, but these hidden emotions emerge in one way or another, sometimes in puzzling behaviors that may affect their learning. The wise adult instructor pays attention to these behaviors and their possible underlying causes. Even if you are powerless to change your learners' attitudes, your awareness of them will help you take the appropriate steps to optimize their learning. You have important ideas and skills to impart, so why settle for less than the best training you can deliver?

## The Best Way to Teach Adults

Jim has spent time as a family-life educator, college professor, staff development specialist, pastor, private workshop leader, and trainer of adult instructors. He has spent a year in China teaching English to university students and faculty. The basics of *Teach With Style* emerged over many years as he turned into a participant-observer, studying other learners' reactions as well as his own. He noted some important and consistent patterns. These insights and discoveries sometimes came from joyful learning successes as well as from some miserable failures. The model presented in this book has been adapted from an earlier version designed specifically for educators of early childhood professionals. Jim decided it was time to expand and present the model to a wider audience of adult instructors, with Lynn's help.

As for Lynn, she was first exposed to teaching adults while on special assignment with her employer at the time, Northwest Airlines. After serving airline passengers at 30,000 feet, she became qualified as a certified facilitator and went on to teach various subjects, from FAA-mandated requalification, to new service procedures, to leadership skills. While a lot of what Lynn taught was highly scripted, she found ways to modify her delivery to make classes enjoyable for the participants, and discovered that there was more to adult learning than just standing in front of the room and lecturing. Lynn currently teaches how to organize and deliver great speeches and presentations. She met Jim at a chapter meeting of the American Society for Training & Development. They discovered their common philosophy of and passion for classroom training, and Jim gave her a copy of the original *Teach With Style* to read. Lynn studied and embraced the model Jim had created, as it paralleled her own ideas, and added her wisdom to the mix.

Combined, we have been teaching adults for more than 70 years. Here we present the essentials of teaching adults in four unique instructor styles, and for each style we include five strategies for optimizing learning. This model has been used for more than 10 years, and our students have found it to be an accurate depiction of how they best learn. We thank the many adult instructors who have helped refine and expand it for your use in serving your adult learners.

We invite you to learn this method and use it to teach what you love to teach. You may embrace it as *the* way you teach, or you can simply use it to augment your other approaches. Our goal in writing this book is to challenge you to continually improve the way you teach. Both you and your learners will benefit from your willingness to change and grow as an instructor.

# 1. The Teach With Style Model

How many instructors or facilitators are charismatic, engaging, dynamic, and riveting speakers? Most of us are dedicated, ordinary adult instructors who nonetheless have important subjects to teach. The model presented in this book is a simple, clear, and proven approach to effective adult instruction that makes it unnecessary to be a powerful orator. It contains valuable guidelines that will help you teach anything well. You will learn techniques for teaching; but more importantly, you will learn to manage the dynamics of the teaching and learning process in order to support growth and lasting change in your adult learners.

## Two Common Instructor Errors

To meet the challenge of teaching adults, you need to be aware of and avoid making two common instructor errors. First, instructors tend to teach the way *they* best learn, and second, instructors tend to teach the way they were taught. For example, if you are a visual learner, you will use pictures and diagrams. If you are an auditory learner, you will teach by talking. Second, you may tend to emulate instructors whom you have found effective, and in doing so, you may not adapt and be flexible when it is necessary. In this book, you will learn to balance four different instructor styles, so that your delivery stays fresh, flexible, and customizable for different audiences.

## Continual Improvement

The model in this book promotes continual improvement. It will help you look closely at your teaching styles and seek ways to change and improve. If you use the model, it does not mean you have to give up your unique qualities as an instructor. You do not need a complete makeover—you just need to keep improving. The tools throughout the book are designed to help you identify your strengths and build on them. At the same time, you must work on the styles and strategies that you use least in order to develop a more balanced and flexible approach.

## Respond to the Diversity of Your Learners

Adult participants bring their personal histories with them to class. Their unique backgrounds and experiences influence how they learn and what they know. Instructors must make their education programs relevant, appropriate, and anti-biased to respond to such factors as gender, age, ability, language, ethnicity, and spirituality. Our pluralistic society provides us with a great learning opportunity as we exchange unique outlooks and solutions to problems of life and work. Instructors must build learning bridges or risk becoming disseminators of stale or useless knowledge. The goal of this book is to teach you to appreciate and respond to the diversity of your learners so that everyone learns well.

## The Four Instructor Styles

Throughout this book, we will be referring to four instructor styles used to teach adult learners effectively. The four instructor styles are based on our theory about how adults learn best. That is, instruction must be *systematic*, *stimulating*, *spontaneous*, and *safe* to be effective for adult learners. When you apply these four styles in your instructional design, greater learning will result. Each style is equally important, and so each must be applied in a balanced way.

### Systematic

Adults learn best when they participate in well-planned programs designed cooperatively with them. Therefore, the instructor should follow a logically and collaboratively designed plan. This is the *systematic instructor style*. The systematic style uses a logical plan that involves the following steps:

- Assess and define needs.
- Set clear learning objectives.
- Design training that is aligned with the objectives.
- Deliver training that is aligned with the objectives and meets learners' expectations.
- Evaluate the results of your program.

Adults respond to well-ordered instruction. We believe that learning takes place with less resistance when learners are not bogged down trying to figure out what's going on and what the objectives of the program are. You should involve the participants in the planning process as much as possible. If it is not possible to fully engage them in the planning process, you can still solicit their ideas and feedback before and during the sessions.

## Stimulating

We have found it helpful and more productive to interact with participants during training programs by using various methods and techniques that challenge participants to change. This is the *stimulating instructor style*.

Adults need to be encouraged to feel, think, and behave in new ways. As participants find their old ideas challenged, they may become resistant to new ideas. Training methods must be active and engaging so that the experience has real and lasting impact. The stimulating instructor style helps learners discover meaningful solutions for life and work, so that they walk away confident, excited, and prepared to apply the new skills and behaviors taught in class.

## Spontaneous

We have found that our adult students learn best when they have freedom in exploring and testing out their new knowledge and skills. Therefore, the instructor should encourage exploration and application of the content when learners are ready to engage in it. This is the *spontaneous instructor style*.

The spontaneous style is the opposite of the systematic style. The spontaneous experience is valuable for adults because it leads to inventiveness and childlike creativity, and diminishes judgmental responses. As adults, we seldom experience that kind of liberation in the classroom. The spontaneous experience includes humor, fun, creative expression, storytelling, risk taking, and meditative reflection. These impromptu moments in the classroom can push learning beyond the confines of an agenda or conventional training methods. Spontaneous explorations of the training material can become turning points in the understanding and personal growth of individual learners.

When balanced with a logical plan, allowing time for participants to explore and discover creates a milieu for creativity and learning. We know where we are headed, so side trips to follow learner interests are feasible without getting too far afield. Allowing a group to dream up the answers to questions is sometimes better than looking for calculated responses. Laughter is refreshing and cleansing and often leads to innovation. We need to see problems in a new light in order to make changes. Many instructors want to keep tight control of the schedule, so allowing these moments may not be easy. Freedom to explore often serves the participants well, however.

## Safe

We have discovered that adults learn best when they are in a safe, trust-filled learning environment. Therefore, the instructor should create a safe learning place for participants. This is the *safe instructor style*.

The safe instructor style is the opposite of the stimulating style. A safe environment includes adequate arrangements for creature comforts, such as rest rooms, appetizing drinks and snacks, adequate breaks, and a comfortable room arrangement.

Participants feel safe when they know they will not be put on the spot, exposed, pressured, or manipulated, and when they play a part in how the learning experience proceeds. Participants also feel safe when they are allowed to interact with and ask questions of the instructor and other participants.

Safety means that a participant's ideas may be challenged, but there is respect for individual differences and points of view. Make it clear to adult participants that they may choose not to participate in any part of the program if it poses undue risk or discomfort, and then provide alternate activities if necessary, or encourage participants to suggest a compromise plan. The basic goal of the safe instructor style is to help people transition into learning and remain open and relaxed in the learning environment. This begins even before learners arrive, and it should continue throughout the experience.

The characteristics of the four instructor styles (summarized in Table 1-1) will help you grasp the basic idea of each style. Each style can meet the needs of adult learners and enable them to learn in the way that is best for them. In chapters to follow, you will learn strategies and tactics to use that support each style.

The best instruction is equally safe, stimulating, systematic, and spontaneous. Proper balance of these four styles is demonstrated in chapter 6 with a sample workshop called "Lead With Style."

## Table 1-1. Characteristics of Instructor Styles

| **Systematic Instructor Style** | **Spontaneous Instructor Style** |
|---|---|
| Follow a logically and collaboratively designed plan. | Encourage exploration, surprise, and unpredictability. |
| • Logical | • Unpredictable |
| • Clear agenda | • Exploration |
| • Stated objective | • Free expression |
| • Behavioral outcome | • Imagination |
| • Orderly | • Creative |
| • Clear | • Artistry |
| • Sensible | • Poetry |
| • Planned | • Music |
| • Purposeful | • Drama |
| • Obtainable goals | • Surprise |
| • Sequential | • Humor |
| • No loose ends | • Risk taking |
| • Predictable | • Wildness |
| **Stimulating Instructor Style** | **Safe Instructor Style** |
| Use active learning approaches and challenge participants to change. | Create a safe learning place for participants. |
| • Challenging | • Comfortable |
| • Provocative | • Peaceful |
| • Dynamic | • Pleasant |
| • Active | • Accepting |
| • Exciting | • Relaxed |
| • Energetic | • Calm |
| • Motivating | • Trusting |
| • Innovative | • Open |
| • Creative tension | • Restful |
| • Progressive | • Mellow |
| • Inspirational | • Protective |
| • Electric | • Harmonious |
| • Lively | • Responsive |

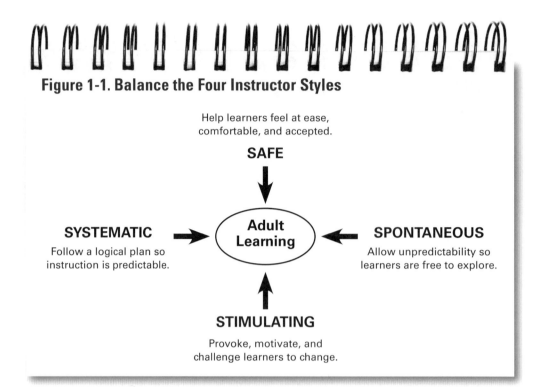

**Figure 1-1. Balance the Four Instructor Styles**

## Instructor Strategies and Learning Activities

The four instructor styles are the fundamental, non-negotiable conditions for ensuring your success as a teacher of adults. You might imagine the instructor strategies as the building blocks for each instructor style. Each strategy guides the selection of the specific tools and tactics you use to teach.

Table 1-2 provides a quick look at the instructor styles and strategies as well as a quick reference to plan training.

The more you use strategies from each of the instructor style categories, the better. You will find that you tend to use some strategies more often than you do others. The strategies you seldom use will be the ones you need to practice and improve. You probably have a natural tendency to employ certain styles and strategies over others, so work on the ones that take you out of your comfort zone. Inexperienced instructors may need to do much work. More seasoned instructors may need to break longtime habits or simply "tune up" their current techniques.

Your instruction style takes shape through the learning activities you use. The most effective instructors use a broad range of tools and tactics. They must be sensitive observers who are able to adjust their instruction to the unique and diverse needs of adult learners. This kind of instruction results in participants who are motivated and open to learning new skills, concepts, and behaviors.

## Table 1-2. Balance Instructor Styles With 20 Strategies

| Use this style: | Because: | By using this style you can: |
|---|---|---|
| **SYSTEMATIC** Set shared objectives; plan for agreed-upon results, and measure success. | Adults are more likely to change when they participate in well-planned programs designed cooperatively. | 1. Collaborate with learners as you plan. 2. Assess participant learning needs and styles. 3. Set clear, meaningful objectives. 4. Plan to reach your objectives. 5. Evaluate your plan. |
| **STIMULATING** Actively challenge adults to think, change, and grow. | Adults will be able to make positive changes when they encounter ideas presented in interesting and lively ways. | 6. Present information in interesting, useful ways. 7. Use active learning approaches. 8. Encourage creativity. 9. Help participants solve real problems. 10. Help participants to practice their learning. |
| **SPONTANEOUS** Plan and allow for play, humor, and surprise in the learning experience. | Adults need opportunity and permission to try out new ways of seeing and behaving to break free from old patterns. | 11. Help participants tell their stories. 12. Make it funny, make it fun. 13. Use imagination and the arts. 14. Allow for risk taking. 15. Take time to reflect. |
| **SAFE** Create comfort zones for adults to take risks in learning. | Adults need a safe, trust-filled learning environment in order to let go of the old and embrace the new. | 16. Help participants feel at home. 17. Let participants know what to expect. 18. Help participants get acquainted. 19. Keep time commitments. 20. Build trust and openness. |

## How This Book Is Organized

This book is divided into eight chapters. The four styles with their respective strategies and learning activities are presented in chapters 2 through 5. In these chapters, you will learn the 20 instructor strategies and more than 120 "take-and-do" ideas and learning activities to help you teach effectively.

In Chapter 6, "Planning for Balanced Instruction," you will learn how to balance the four styles through a sample workshop designed for managers called "Lead With Style."

Chapter 7, "Practical Application of the Model," will show you how to implement the model. It traces the process from planning through implementation for an actual workshop on presentation methods. It shows how specific learning activities can be selected to provide an interesting and useful program for participants.

Chapter 8, "Plan Your Continual Improvement," presents tools and inventories for planning your continual improvement as an instructor.

The four instructor styles—systematic, stimulating, spontaneous, and safe—address the four ways in which adults learn best. You can effectively teach adult learners by applying these four styles in a balanced way in your instructional design. Now that you have a sense of the whole, let's turn to a discussion of each individual style.

# 2. The Systematic Instructor Style

Adults learn more when they participate in well-planned programs that are cooperatively designed. Systematic instruction is characterized by shared objectives, a program that reaches the objectives, and evaluation of progress toward the objectives. The systematic strategies, learning activities, and tactics in this chapter will help you design instruction so it flows logically from learning needs to learning outcomes.

Systematic strategies include the following:

- Collaborate with learners as you plan.
- Assess participant learning needs and styles.
- Set clear, meaningful objectives.
- Plan to reach your objectives.
- Evaluate your plan.

##  Systematic Strategy 1: Collaborate With Learners as You Plan

Collaborative instruction should be well-targeted and flexible in meeting participant needs. When possible, consult directly with the learners as you plan. Involve learners before and during the course of instruction to make the experience relevant to their needs. Be willing to shift the program, when warranted, and openly share the consequences of doing so with your learners.

Learners are more likely to learn when they take ownership of the learning experience. In George Lakey's *Facilitating Group Learning: Strategies for Success With Diverse Adult Learners*, the author makes a strong case for ownership of objectives, stating, "Participants cannot become powerful learners while coasting on the objectives set out in the curriculum. Each participant needs to state what she or he wants to learn, concretely and realistically."

Meet directly with a group of learners early on to involve them in planning. Teaching is a partnership between participant and teacher. Ideally, you will get to know your learners before and during the course of instruction so you can plan together for the best instructional fit.

Do not be afraid to relinquish some of your control (or to hang on where needed)—just be clear about which aspects of the instructional experience are negotiable and which are not. In some circumstances very little is negotiable (for example, in a highly structured academic setting) and in others the sky is the limit (for example, in an informal community class). Make sure you are not holding on to control just for your own comfort. Listen to your learners and modify your instruction to meet their needs.

The following tactics reinforce the systematic instructor style.

## Tactic 1.1: Learning Team Approach

**Purpose:** Facilitate self-directed group learning.

**Description:** Instruct the learners to select members for these roles: the leader acts as facilitator for the planning; the recorder acts as the team's memory; and the observer stays in the background and provides information on how the group is working. The instructor also stays in the background and makes herself available to consult and guide when needed. The participant facilitator leads this six-step process:

1. Discuss and list the needs and interests of the group.

2. From this list, choose those that are most vital to the group and more clearly define and prioritize them.

3. Use this list to make a learning schedule of topics and set learning objectives for each.

4. Discuss and list all the resources and learning techniques for reaching each objective. Assign a topic to each member or teams of members.

5. Each member or team takes a topic to research and present to the group.

6. The instructor acts as consultant to each teacher or teaching team.

## Tactic 1.2: Representative Group

**Purpose:** Collaborate with a small group of representatives.

**Description:** Learners are selected to act as representatives because they are able to reflect the larger groups' thoughts about learning needs. The instructor meets with the representative group one or more times to conduct the assessment. Prepare open-ended questions but be ready to follow the direction in which the group process leads. When you feel you have a good grasp of what is needed, present your conclusions to the group for their comments. When the group agrees with your assessment, you may ask them to return to the larger group they represent to see if there is a fit and, if there is, proceed with planning the curriculum.

## Tactic 1.3: On-the-Spot Collaboration

**Purpose:** Provides the opportunity to collaborate when time is short or when there is no opportunity to gather information or meet with learners or their representatives.

**Description:** If you are not able to collaborate prior to the session, you should at least spend some time determining the learners' needs and expectations at the beginning of the class so you can modify your plans to better meet their needs. Tell learners what is planned and what the parameters are for adjusting the method and content of the instruction. Solicit opinions and ideas from the group and let them know what is and is not realistic. Take whatever time you have available for this—it will be time well spent.

## Tactic 1.4: Interviews With Managers

**Purpose:** Allows an instructor to collaborate with managers during session planning, so that the learning objectives are validated and managers support the application of learning back on the job.

**Description:** Make the effort to talk with decision makers when you plan instruction. Get their input on the learning objectives and methods. Their attitudes about the training and the support (or lack thereof) they offer to learners can make or break the learning experience.

## Tactic 1.5: On-the-Spot Interviews

**Purpose:** Allows the instructor to quickly assess learners' needs and interests and collaborate with them in planning.

**Description:** The instructor can quickly assess learning needs in conversations with learners as they arrive. This is particularly effective in conference workshops where the instructor has little time to collaborate with learners on content or methods. Prepare questions in advance and meet individually with learners as they arrive to get their input. Make a list of your findings and present this to the rest of the class when they are assembled.

If your class extends over several sessions, you can plan to question learners several times to see if they are getting what they need and if they understand your instruction. Make periodic reports to the class and modify your instruction accordingly.

## Tactic 1.6: Small Group In-Session Collaboration

**Purpose:** Provides a method for collaboration after a session has begun.

**Description:** Sometimes you may feel you have not targeted your instruction as well as you could have. It's not too late to collaborate and make adjustments. Take a break from learning and explain to the learners that you need more input from them to help you teach more effectively. Divide the class into small groups and have each group look over the syllabus (objectives and agenda) and provide feedback to you about it. Some formats for small group work include:

- Take 10 minutes in your groups and design the ideal workshop on your topic.

- In your small groups, decide which topics are most important to you. Then describe the ways in which you would like to learn about them. Be ready to report in 15 minutes.

- Take some time to look over the syllabus for the class (objectives and agenda for the workshop) and make notes. Meet with your small group and suggest improvements. Be prepared to explain and discuss your suggestions.

## Tactic 1.7: In-Class Feedback

**Purpose:** Solicit expectations from the group at any time in the training event.

**Description:** Arrange the learners in several small groups of two to five persons each. Have groups answer these three questions: How are we feeling about this session? What do we wish would happen? What do you wish would not happen? Groups report and you help them clarify each point as necessary. Give each group a marker and flipchart to jot notes for sharing with the larger group. (Anonymity can be maintained by the presenter leaving the room and then flipchart sheets are traded between groups.) Let the learners know which of their wishes can and can't be met. Contract with the group to meet agreed-on wishes. See also, chapter 5, Tactic 18.6.

## Systematic Strategy 2: Assess Participant Learning Needs and Styles

Instruction should be based on participant needs, interests, and styles of learning. Diversity issues must be considered. Pay attention to the accessibility of facilities, special learning needs, and anti-bias concerns. Determine how learners best receive, integrate, and express information. Consider combining different assessment methods for more accurate results.

The following tactics reinforce the systematic learning style.

## Tactic 2.1: Inventory

**Purpose:** Helps instructors gather information that can be easily and quickly analyzed.

**Description:** An inventory is a written assessment received directly from the learners or management. Questionnaires, checklists, or surveys are common forms of inventories. These inventories ask questions about needs and interests of learners and then the data is analyzed in preparation for instruction. Instruction is designed around the most prevalent needs, interests, or learning styles. The advantages of inventories are that they are usually easy to administer, inexpensive, take little time, and are confidential. Disadvantages can include a low return rate, unreliable results, or results that are difficult to interpret.

In Worksheets 2-1 and 2-2, we have provided some samples of inventories that can be used by instructors to assess learning styles in classes or workshops. Instructors can distribute them to learners in advance of a workshop, tally the information, and adjust their teaching strategies according to the results. Learners can also fill them out at the beginning of a workshop; a tally can be made during a break and then adjustments made for the rest of the learning experience. In addition, these can be taken by instructors themselves to gain some information about their own learning styles.

Worksheet 2-1 is a learning style inventory that examines the best ways learners receive, integrate, and demonstrate knowledge and skills.

Worksheet 2-2 may also be helpful in determining the learning styles of your learners based on the Teach With Style model.

### Worksheet 2-1. How Do You Learn Best?

*The learning cycle includes 1) receiving, 2) exploring and integrating, and 3) demonstrating competence in knowledge, skill, or understanding in a particular subject area. Check three to five methods in each category that suit you best while learning.*

**How do you best RECEIVE knowledge, skill, or understanding?**
__ Stories, anecdotes, illustrations
__ Charts, graphs
__ Lectures
__ Short talks, lecturettes
__ Question and answer sessions
__ Reading
__ Films, videos
__ Logical sequencing

__ Bits and pieces
__ Surprise and humor
__ Lots of repetition
__ Demonstrations
__ Case studies
__ Simulations and games
__ Personal coaching/mentoring
__ Peer learning
__ Computer programs
__ Home study
__ Classroom
__ Self-directed learning
__ Flipcharts

__ _____

__ _____

__ _____

**How do you like to EXPLORE AND INTEGRATE knowledge, skill, or understanding?**

__ Small group discussion
__ Large group discussion
__ Write a report
__ Do a research project
__ Small group assignments
__ Problem solving, puzzles, and challenges
__ Artwork, drawing, sculpting, and so on
__ Dialogue with one other person
__ Simulations and games
__ Demonstrations
__ Debates
__ Role playing
__ Guided imagery
__ Journaling
__ Meditating, pondering

__ _____

__ _____

__ _____

**How do you like to DEMONSTRATE your learning?**

__ Take a written test
__ Essay test
__ True/false, multiple choice
__ Photo essay
__ Live demonstration
__ Group project
__ Make a statistical chart
__ Keep a journal

__ Give a talk
__ Conduct an experiment
__ Teach it to someone else
__ Engage in a debate or discussion
__ Produce a video
__ Dramatic presentation or skit
__ Present to a small group
__ Do a mind map
__ Role play

__ _____

__ _____

__ _____

**My Learning Style**
Reflect on your responses and write a brief summary of how you like to learn.

_____

_____

_____

## Tactic 2.2: Interview

**Purpose:** Helps the instructor acquire in-depth opinions of participant needs.

**Description:** Interviews can be done individually or in a group. They can be a follow-up to other needs assessments or serve as a stand-alone method. The interviewer(s) may ask some of the same questions as in an inventory, and then ask follow-up questions to clarify answers. Interviews provide a precise diagnosis of participant needs and a face-to-face analysis, allowing assessment of feelings and opinions as well as facts. It provides a more personal touch. However, interviews are time-consuming and may not provide a very broad picture. Confidentiality is not possible.

## Tactic 2.3: Inquiry

**Purpose:** Provides a systematic analysis of information or data that is already available.

**Description:** Analyze complaints from customers, statistics on staff turnover or accidents, staff comments, supervisor evaluations, and so forth. There is much information to be found in organizational records that can reveal learning needs. You can follow up your analysis of these data with inventories or interviews. Make sure confidentiality is maintained and proper authorizations are secured. Inquiries are convenient, do not take up workers' time, and use objective rather than subjective information. However, information is only as good as the data available. Inquiries also do not identify root causes of skill or knowledge gaps.

## Worksheet 2-2. Learner Styles Inventory

*Check the boxes that best represent your favorite ways to learn. Add up check marks to get learning style scores.*

| Learner Style | Learning Activity | Learner Style | Learning Activity |
|---|---|---|---|
| SYSTEMATIC | ☐ Case studies<br>☐ Charts and graphs<br>☐ Clear goals and objectives<br>☐ Well-organized lectures<br>☐ Computer programs<br>☐ Well-outlined topics<br>☐ Expert panel discussion<br>☐ Written material or handouts<br>☐ Structured classroom seating<br>☐ Workbooks<br>☐ Written, objective tests<br><br>**Systematic Style Score:** | SPONTANEOUS | ☐ Drawing, sculpting, and so on<br>☐ Drama or role playing<br>☐ Creating and inventing<br>☐ Guided imagination<br>☐ Journaling<br>☐ Fun activities and games<br>☐ Meditating<br>☐ Mind mapping<br>☐ Storytelling<br>☐ Surprise and humor<br>☐ Taking risks<br>☐ Poetry and music<br><br>**Spontaneous Style Score:** |
| STIMULATING | ☐ Active learning approaches<br>☐ Debates<br>☐ Demonstrations<br>☐ Dynamic short presentations<br>☐ Clear principles<br>☐ Group projects<br>☐ Examples and illustrations<br>☐ Time to practice<br>☐ Question and answer period<br>☐ Solving real-life problems<br>☐ Teaching others<br>☐ Guided group discussions<br><br>**Stimulating Style Score:** | SAFE | ☐ Friendly instructor<br>☐ Get acquainted/warm-up exercises<br>☐ Good refreshments<br>☐ Group projects<br>☐ Know what will happen<br>☐ Mentoring<br>☐ Comfortable learning space<br>☐ Peer learning<br>☐ Personal coaching<br>☐ Relaxed atmosphere<br>☐ Self-study programs<br>☐ Small group discussion<br><br>**Safe Style Score:** |

List some other ways you like to learn:

_____
_____
_____
_____
_____

What advice would you give the instructor(s) to make the learning most effective and enjoyable for you?

_____
_____
_____
_____
_____

## Tactic 2.4: Direct Observation

**Purpose:** Provides concrete examples of learning knowledge and ability.

**Description:** Observation takes great skill and a clear purpose on the part of an observer or facilitator. The observer uses clear-cut criteria to observe learners while they demonstrate knowledge and skill either in simulated or real-life conditions. The observer determines what instruction is needed based on the analysis. Direct observations provide a clear diagnosis of participant needs. However, they require a skilled assessment facilitator, are time consuming, and the mere fact of being observed may influence the behavior of the person being observed.

## Tactic 2.5: Examination

**Purpose:** Determines learning needs through testing learners.

**Description:** The examiner administers written, oral, or experiential tests to learners to determine their level of knowledge, skill, or understanding. The best tests are those that have been certified by research and are proven to accurately assess learners. Many such tests are available in many fields of learning. Examinations provide an objective measure of needs or learning styles. However, many people are not good test-takers and therefore their performance on the test may inaccurately reflect their level of skill or knowledge. Examinations may also be expensive to administer.

## Tactic 2.6: Informal Discussions

**Purpose:** Provides an informal way for learners to communicate their needs and interests to the instructor.

**Description:** Informal discussion with a whole class or small groups before and during instruction can be helpful for getting a picture of participant needs, interests, and learning styles. The "I Wish…" exercise found in Tactic 18.6 is an example of this. The idea is to pose an assessment question for discussion and let the group respond to it. The instructor adjusts the instruction based on this information. This tactic allows the instructor to gain fresh insight into the learners' needs that may go beyond stated objectives. It also gives participants a sense of ownership of the learning experience. However, the content may be emotionally driven, or some more dominant participants may assert their needs over those less willing or able to express their needs.

### Tactic 2.7: Listing and Voting

**Purpose:** Allows members of a class or workshop to help determine content and methods.

**Description:** The instructor may bring a defined curriculum and set methods, but allow for modifications. Begin by listing all the options (topics for study, methods of learning, and so forth). Next let members vote on the options they think will be most important to them. Let learners place colored dots (each color has a value) next to their favorite item on a flipchart as a way to "vote." In this way, learners "spend" their dots as they choose. Learners may also first "lobby" for their own choices. Then the votes are cast. The instructor uses the results of the voting to determine or adjust course content and methods. Voting allows each person to make known their needs and interests in a democratic way. However, when the majority rules, the minority opinions get overlooked and this may lead to the disengagement of those who lose out.

## Systematic Strategy 3: Set Clear, Meaningful Objectives

Carefully formulated and articulated objectives should be based on the instructor's assessment of the needs and interests of learners. Make these objectives available for review. An instructor should be able to say specifically what learners can expect to gain from taking the class or workshop session. Sometimes very specific behavioral or performance objectives are best, for example, "After viewing a video on employee safety, you will be able to identify at least five safety problems in a photograph of a work setting."

Clear objectives help adult learners know whether your instruction will meet their needs and expectations. Clear objectives make it possible to know if your instruction is on target throughout the learning experience (Mager, 1997). How often have you sat in a workshop wondering where things were headed? Adults will often allow a class to drift rather than risk challenging the teacher. It is fair and prudent to have clear learning objectives to guide your instruction.

Objectives are like benefits you might gain by buying a product or service. As you plan, think how your learners will gain from participation in your workshop or course. Think of your learners as customers. Teaching is rarely thought of as an exchange of learners' time, energy, and money for knowledge. However, learners (and their organizations) should tangibly benefit from their investment.

The following tactics for creating clear, meaningful objectives reinforce the systematic instructor style.

### Tactic 3.1: Reversing the Problem or Need

**Purpose:** Presents an easy and useful way to create objectives.

**Description:** One way to craft an objective is to turn a problem or need into a positive statement. If your participants don't know how to organize speeches, your goal will be "Participants will know how to organize a speech using a mind-mapping tool." Just reverse the need or problem by stating its opposite. If you can state your problem, you can state your objective. See Worksheet 2-3 to practice this.

### Worksheet 2-3. Turning a Problem Into an Objective Statement

*Use the examples below to practice writing an objective statement from the problem statement. Note: Cover up the last column as you practice and then check your work.*

| Problem | Fill in your objective statement | Examples |
|---|---|---|
| My students don't know how to process insurance claims. | | • The students will be able to list the standard steps in processing insurance claims.<br>• You will be able to process insurance claims using the guidelines provided. |
| Our employees have not learned to use the new network email. | | • All the employees will be able to email using the new system.<br>• You will be able to use the new network email system. |
| Our managers have set goals but don't know how to develop action steps to reach them. | | • The managers will be able to define action steps for each organizational goal.<br>• The managers will know how to reach goals by listing related action steps. |

## Tactic 3.2: Three Levels of Learning—Understanding, Knowledge, and Skill

**Purpose:** Presents three ways to state objectives.

**Description:** Learning objectives can address learners' understanding, knowledge, or skill. Use Table 2-1 as a guide for writing clear objectives that address one (or more) of these three elements.

### Table 2-1. Three Types of Learning Objectives

| Learning Objective | Examples |
|---|---|
| **Understand:** the ability to perceive the meaning of something, explain a cause, or be aware of something | • The student will explain how each feature of our product meets the needs of a customer.<br>• Describe ways that a manager might motivate his employees.<br>• Given three customer service scenarios, explain how and why the customer service representative could have been more effective. |
| **Know:** the ability to recall facts and principles and apply them in solving problems | • Identify at least five ways to ensure all members of your team are engaged in project planning.<br>• List the ways to stop bleeding and explain the proper use of the tourniquet.<br>• Write a brief history of our retail development and name key people in its development.<br>• Name and describe five "best practice" principles covered in our course textbook. |
| **Develop skill:** the ability to do something well, to perform tasks with efficiency and effectiveness resulting in a process or product that meets certain standards | • Demonstrate the proper use of a fire extinguisher.<br>• Delegate appropriate tasks and follow up with supportive coaching.<br>• Use desktop publishing software to create professional publications. |

## Tactic 3.3: Process Objectives

**Purpose:** Guides your instructional design.

**Description:** In addition to *content* objectives that include understanding, knowledge, and skill, you can use *process* objectives to meet the instructional method standards you want to reach. Do you want to spend at least 25 percent of the time at the beginning of a workshop for warm-up and getting acquainted? This is a process objective. Do you want plenty of participation in the session? Do you want to develop a mentoring system in your childcare classes? These are process objectives. Process objectives are usually not published—they are your personal guidelines that describe how you instruct. When you work toward greater balance in using all the instructor styles and strategies, you will want to have process objectives to help you plan improvement in your instruction.

## Tactic 3.4: Personal Objectives

**Purpose:** Helps learners individualize learning outcomes.

**Description:** Improve the effectiveness of your instruction by allowing learners to identify their own personal learning objectives. This can be done in the beginning, middle, or end of a workshop, conference, or class. Ask learners to write a personalized objective they want to reach as a result of the learning event. For example, in a course on developing good working relationships a student may write, "I want to be able to meet and remember the names of all my colleagues." Have learners write objectives at the beginning to help them focus and take advantage of the experiences ahead, or do this later on to allow learners an opportunity to become familiar with the subject matter so more precise personal objectives can be set. At the end of the event, you can send learners away with personal objectives to achieve as they apply the learning.

Some ways to help learners set personal objectives include:

- Give each participant a card and ask them to write objectives on one side and a method to reach them on the other.

- Establish partners (or small groups) to work as a team to help each other set personal objectives. The partners or team members can help each other throughout the workshop or in the future to keep the commitments to reach these objectives.

- At the end of a learning event, learners write objectives on a card with their email or telephone numbers listed (if they are comfortable doing this). These can be handed to another person for follow-up or distributed randomly with instructions to contact the person in three months to check on progress. They can also be slipped into self-addressed envelopes and sent to learners by the instructor.

- Learners can be asked to write "self-contracts" by recording objectives they wish to achieve. Another learner can sign as a witness to help strengthen the resolve.

## Tactic 3.5: Getting Agreement on Objectives

**Purpose:** Form a partnership for learning.

**Description:** The process of getting agreement on objectives between the instructor and learners may be a formal or highly informal arrangement. Sometimes the simple process of signing up for a course or a conference can be considered agreement. In a one-hour class on how to be a better listener, there is an assumption that the instructor will teach an introduction only on that topic. If, on the other hand, the instructor only covers introductory material in an all-day workshop, learners will feel cheated. Publish specific objectives so learners will know what to expect.

The following methods can be used to reach agreement with learners:

- State objectives and allow learners to vote on or rank the ones they most want to achieve.

- Ask the learners to review the class objectives; allow learners to raise questions or objections in group discussion. Read each objective and have them simply nod their heads if they agree.

- State the objectives, content, and methods of the class. Call for a break and let those who want to leave exit from the room. Those who remain have agreed with the stated objectives.

- Allow learners to discuss the course syllabus or outline and suggest changes. If none are suggested, you have an agreement. If changes are proposed, renegotiate where reasonable.

- Make a more formal agreement by writing out the objectives and responsibilities of learners and instructors and have each of the parties sign it.

## Tactic 3.6: Publish the Objectives

**Purpose:** Encourages instructors to be clear and open about objectives.

**Description:** Writing objectives is important. All involved are able to track progress toward them if they are published. Here are some ways to publish objectives:

- General objectives should be published at the first announcement of a learning event so learners can choose knowledgeably.

- Publish instructional objectives on a handout or on the first page of participant materials.

- Write them on a flipchart or projected image. This allows you to make changes and modifications.

- Draw boxes next to each objective so you can check them off as each objective is met.

- Go back over the objectives when you complete the instruction as a means of review for you and the learners.

## Tactic 3.7: Behavioral Outcomes – The G.A.S. Method

**Purpose:** To have an accurate accounting of learning.

**Description:** An objective is a statement from the instructor's point of view. A behavioral outcome describes what the learner will be able to do. There are three parts to a behavioral outcome:

G = the *given* condition for the behavioral requirement

A = what the learner will be *able* to understand, know, or do

S = the *standard* the behavior must meet to be successful.

Here is a humorous introduction to writing behavioral outcomes. It shows the difference between an *objective* and a *behavioral* outcome:

Objectives:

- You will be able to skin potatoes effectively.

- You will be able to run faster than a speeding bullet.

- You will be able to leap tall buildings in a single bound.

Behavioral Outcomes:

- Given 10 potatoes and a paring knife (G), the trainee will be able to peel the potatoes (A) in five minutes without leaving any skin attached (S).

- Given a clear day with no breeze (G), the participant will be able to reach the finish line (A) before the bullet, which is fired from the starting gun (S).

- Given a superman suit and flying instructions (G), the student will leave 4th Avenue in downtown Seattle and pass over the Columbia Tower (A) in a single bodily motion and land safely on 5th Avenue (S).

You can practice writing behavioral outcomes in Worksheet 2-4.

## Worksheet 2-4. Practice Writing Behavioral Outcomes

*Here are three objectives. Covering up the bottom of this chart, turn these objectives into behavioral outcomes.*

**Objective 1:** Identify the elements of a good presentation.
Write a Behavioral Outcome:

_____

_____

**Objective 2:** List the benefits of the new line of men's underwear.
Write a Behavioral Outcome:

_____

_____

**Objective 3:** Wash your hands properly before assisting a patient.
Write a Behavioral Outcome:

_____

_____

**Answers:**
1. After viewing a video of a presentation with at least 20 good elements, write down the elements that made it good, identifying at least 15 elements.
2. Given a handout and demonstration by the instructor, be able to state all of the benefits of the new line of men's underwear in a casual conversational manner to a role-playing partner.
3. Given a sink and soap, be able to wash your hands so that no germ residue remains, as determined by an ultraviolet light.

## Tactic 3.8: A Standard Objective – Enjoy Learning

**Purpose:** Reminds instructors to make learning enjoyable.

**Description:** Always put "enjoy learning" at the end of your list of objectives. Learners will be very pleased and relieved that you are going to make this experience enjoyable for them. It is a reminder that, although teaching and learning are hard work, you can still have fun in the process.

## Systematic Strategy 4: Plan to Reach Your Objectives

This strategy supports instruction that is based on, and achieves, the objectives. If necessary, be willing to renegotiate with learners to adjust the program or objectives. When the program is completed, the learners should report and demonstrate in the evaluation process whether they learned what they needed and wanted to learn. For example, if an instructor tells you that you are going to be able to describe the best features of the new automobile model on the showroom floor, that is what you should be able to do by the end of the learning experience. What happens in the instruction should match precisely the objectives or stated purpose.

Your instructional program should flow naturally from your objectives, just as objectives flow naturally from the assessment of needs. An important message of this book is to plan instruction that balances the four styles. Once you are ready to design your instruction, remember to balance the four styles to make it systematic, stimulating, spontaneous, and safe. Make sure you are able to use all the strategies that support those styles.

The following tactics can help you plan to reach your objectives.

## Tactic 4.1: Have an Agenda

**Purpose:** Provides a visual means for keeping on track.

**Description:** An agenda, syllabus, or outline that you and your learners follow keeps things on target. This can be as simple as a list of topics and activities on a flipchart or as formal as a printed agenda. The important thing is to publish the path toward your objectives. Follow it just like you would a map that outlines the route to your destination.

Here is a sample agenda for a two-hour class on being a better listener:

Objectives:

- Understand the importance of listening.
- Know and experience the benefits of listening.
- Improve your listening skills.

Agenda:

| | |
|---|---|
| 7:00 p.m. | Introduction and the importance of listening (lecturette) |
| 7:15 p.m. | Warm-up and getting acquainted (small group activity) |
| 7:30 p.m. | How to listen (handout provided) |
| 8:45 p.m. | How to—and how not to—listen (demonstration) |
| 8:00 p.m. | Listening practice with feedback (small group exercise) |
| 8:45 p.m. | Wrap-up and evaluation |

## Tactic 4.2: Organizing Instruction

**Purpose:** Helps learners take logical steps toward the objectives.

**Description:** Here are some ways to organize instruction:

- Simple to complex. Begin with the simplest aspects of a topic and move toward more complex concepts and skills; for example, a child moves from mounting and balancing a bicycle to steering and braking. In a workshop on listening skills, the instruction begins with some basic skills such as body posture, eye contact, and facial expression, and then moves onto more complex processes like paraphrasing, restating, and summarizing what was said.

- Logical progression. For example, in teaching an introduction to counseling the instructor may begin by covering the current philosophies and practices. Next you may demonstrate or show video examples of particular theoretical methods. This is followed up by students practicing the skills and then receiving feedback.

- Have a beginning, middle, and end. Teaching a class is just like writing an article or book. You begin at the beginning with some kind of introduction, move into the body of the text, and then come to a conclusion.

For some other ways of organizing instruction, see Tactic 6.2 in chapter 3.

## Tactic 4.3: Renegotiate as Needed

**Purpose:** Keeps instruction on track.

**Description:** Periodically check to see if you are on target. If you find you are not reaching your objectives, you may need to renegotiate them. The problem may stem from having made an incorrect assessment of learners' needs; in this case you need to reassess. Or the source of the problem may be incorrect objective statements; you need to restate the objectives. The problem may be in using the wrong methods; you will need to change your methods. Do not be hesitant to readjust and renegotiate—you want to reach the right objectives on behalf of your learners.

## Tactic 4.4: Actively Encourage Learning

**Purpose:** Reminds instructors to actively encourage learning to reach objectives.

**Description:** Use every moment to create conditions that encourage learners to actively take responsibility for their own learning. Strive to spark curiosity, a search for truth, and continual improvement. Here are some suggestions to accomplish this:

- Ask more questions, give fewer answers.
- Form study/work groups; encourage cooperative learning.
- Be slow to speak—do not be so quick to make your points; draw out the points from your learners.

- Point the way—do not lead the learners but set them in the right direction.
- Model curiosity and truth-seeking. Let learners in on your quest for answers.
- Promote mutual discovery and less structured teaching through open dialogue.

## Tactic 4.5: Instructor Planning Template

**Purpose:** Balances your instructional planning.

**Description:** Using some kind of template can be very helpful once you have discovered a pattern that works for you. The *Instructor Planning Notes* is a form you can use to plan instruction that balances the four instructor styles (see chapter 6, Worksheet 6-1). This form guides you through a sequence of planning. It begins with the systematic style to set the proper direction for your instruction. Next, you are asked to create learning that is stimulating and challenging. Then you try to find ways to make learning spontaneous and fun, and finally, create plans for helping learners feel comfortable. A template provides a guide so that you don't miss important steps in planning.

## Tactic 4.6: Instructional Module Guide

**Purpose:** Provides a template when planning instruction.

**Description:** Planning can be made easier by dividing your class or workshop into a series of related but separate modules. There are many ways to design these and you may want to design your own. An instructional module guide is a standardized outline you can use when designing lessons. The example in Table 2-2 can help you plan.

## Tactic 4.7: Design Matrix

**Purpose:** Aids in planning instruction.

**Description:** A matrix is a simple visual presentation of your instructional plan. One way to use a matrix is to have the essential elements listed across the top to form the columns (objectives, methods, materials, and so forth). Along the side, list the sequence for each part of your presentation. An example of a matrix is presented in Table 2-3. You can add or modify this design to fit your own particular planning needs. Other examples of a matrix are provided in chapter 7, Tables 7-1 and 7-2.

**Table 2-2. Sample Instructional Module Guide**

☐ Title of the Module: Give it a title that is clever or humorous.

☐ Learning Objectives: List what students will take away from this event—how will they change?

☐ Content Outline for Each Objective: Outline the content needed for each objective and the method of delivery (handout, PowerPoint, lecturette, Socratic questioning, and so on).

☐ Options for Content: What can be left out; what can be added? It is best to plan with more material than less.

☐ Procedures (steps and their sequence): Spell out the exact steps and in what sequence things will happen. Determine the timing for each step.

☐ Options for Procedures: List any changes that could be made depending on the situation. You may or may not need them.

☐ Materials Needed: List everything you'll need to be ready for the module. List the materials and equipment needed for each step in the procedures.

☐ Options for Materials: What if the bulb burns out in the projector; what if you need more handouts than you thought? Be ready to flex.

☐ Evaluation Design: Be ready with a way to measure your success—there should be a way to measure whether you met each objective listed. You may also wish to elicit feedback on your course procedures and content.

##  Systematic Strategy 5: Evaluate Your Plan

This strategy determines the degree to which the learning experience met the objectives, how you might improve future learning experiences, and if further instruction is needed by the learners.

Remember that planning is a process that involves learners in assessing learning needs, setting objectives, and planning to reach them. The last step is checking to see if your plan and your instructional methods worked. Did you reach your objectives? Did learners gain the understanding, knowledge, and skills they needed? How might the instruction be improved? This can happen during the four levels of evaluation (Kirkpatrick, 1994; see Table 2-4). Whether simple or complex, evaluating results is a necessary step to determine and increase your effectiveness.

The following tactics will help you evaluate your instructional plan.

## Table 2-3. Sample Matrix—Business Writing Workshop (Introductory Portion)

| Module Title | Objectives | Methods | Materials | Options/Time | Evaluation |
|---|---|---|---|---|---|
| 1. Introduction and warm-up | Learn session objectives and agenda. | Discussion of objectives; small groups sharing their "writing histories" | Handout describing session objectives and agenda | 20 minutes (five for intro, 10 for small groups, 10 for feedback and instructor comments) | Do learners feel ready to learn to write? |
| 2. The importance of effective business writing | Learn how effective business writing can benefit you. | Lecturette on importance of good writing – humorous and disastrous stories of poor communication | Audiovisual equipment | 30 minutes with Q&A | Do learners know how quality writing can benefit their work? |
| 3. Sample writing exercise | Identify good and bad examples of business writing. | 1. Groups of 3 examine 4 samples of portions of reports. Rank them from best to worst. 2. Feedback and general discussion | Sample sheets, flipchart, pens, and tape | 30 minutes (10 for groups to rank and 20 for feedback and discussion) | Can learners identify good and bad elements of business writing samples? |

## Table 2-4. Measuring Learning Experiences

| Level | Measurement |
|-------|-------------|
| 1 | Determine what the students felt about the experience. Solicit the learners' opinion about the experience. Did they like the instruction and the instructor? How might it be improved? Typically, participants answer questions on an evaluation form after the event. |
| 2 | Determine what the students thought they learned. Solicit the learners' opinions on what they think they learned—was the instruction helpful? Did they learn what they wanted and needed? |
| 3 | Determine if the objectives were met. Solicit the learners' opinions to what extent each of the learning objectives was met. Usually each objective is listed and students are asked to rate them. |
| 4 | Determine precisely what students understand, know, or can do—this is done through testing or demonstrations to determine behavioral outcomes. |

## Tactic 5.1: Questionnaire

**Purpose:** A questionnaire is a quick way to assess learning success.

**Description:** The most typical way to evaluate instruction is through a questionnaire given to learners at the conclusion of an event. A questionnaire is a quick and easy way to evaluate the participants' impressions of the instruction, although it may not be the most accurate. Usually evaluation forms are passed out at the end of an event when adults are getting ready to leave, and so they may respond hurriedly. Nonetheless, some valuable information can be gathered. (An example of a questionnaire is provided in chapter 7, Worksheet 7-1.) Some areas to evaluate through a questionnaire are the following:

- Objectives—to what extent were they achieved?
- Instructional design—was it effective?
- Instructional content—did it meet the need?
- Methods—were they appropriate for the content and the audience?
- Instructor—how could the instructor improve?
- Participant response—was the experience helpful, enjoyable, and engaging?

## Tactic 5.2: Photo or Video Essay

**Purpose:** Provides a visual account of participant accomplishment.

**Description:** Learners take pictures of their work that become a permanent accounting of their accomplishments in the class. This activity promotes creativity and encourages learners to come up with a concrete representation of their work. Learners are asked to accompany their work with verbal or written descriptions on areas for further inquiry.

## Tactic 5.3: Live Demonstrations

**Purpose:** Learners demonstrate learning results.

**Description:** Learners are asked to provide a concrete example of their new learning. A recital is a common demonstration of musical skill. This approach can be easily adapted to any learning. You are asking learners to show what they learned. Math learners can put formulas on a blackboard, childcare learners can show how they conduct storytelling to class members, or marketing learners might demonstrate their ad campaign. If a real-world demonstration is not possible, role playing or simulations can be used. The audience may vary—it may be a group of learners or the instructor alone.

## Tactic 5.4: Journaling

**Purpose:** Provides a written log of learning.

**Description:** A journal can be a handy way of recording learning for classroom discussions, instructor evaluations, or for future reference by learners. A journal can be simple and short or an extensive and complex record of learning. The format can be index cards used to easily organize information or a book to record the flow of thoughts or events.

## Tactic 5.5: Group Project

**Purpose:** Provides for a cooperative evaluation effort.

**Description:** A group project is a way for learners to work together to show evidence of learning. A group project can be used for a short course or workshop or as the culmination of extended course work. The instructor may want to create conditions so all members of a group contribute equally. The instructor can appoint and meet with participant team leaders to accomplish this or meet periodically with the team to assess how learners are working cooperatively.

## Tactic 5.6: Image of Learning

**Purpose:** Uses visual art to communicate learning.

**Description:** Mind mapping, collages, montages, sculptures, diagrams, and models are examples of visual images that show learning. The visual can be evaluated based on well-defined criteria or reactions that are more subjective. The evaluation can be done by class members or by the instructor.

## Tactic 5.7: Group Testing

**Purpose:** Provides a public evaluation with low risk for learners.

**Description:** The instructor constructs a short test based on information taught. Then the test is put on an overhead, computer projector, or whiteboard. An objective test with fill-in answers such as matching or true-and-false questions is best. The instructor presents the test and learners can call out answers for a quick check of accuracy. The test can be repeated until the whole class makes a perfect response. Small groups can take a similar test. You can add spice to this technique by offering prizes for correct answers.

## Tactic 5.8: Participant Teachers

**Purpose:** Uses teaching to demonstrate ability.

**Description:** Have learners teach each other a topic or skill as a means of demonstrating their knowledge or ability. You may have different individuals or groups learn different parts of the subject and teach them to others. Alternatively, you may have everyone learn the same thing and then take turns teaching it again to each other. This is a good way to involve learners as teachers and have them evaluate each other.

For more ideas about evaluation, review the learning activities in the systematic strategy, *Assess Participant Learning Needs and Styles*. You can adapt these methods of assessment for use as methods of evaluation. In addition, look over Worksheet 2-5 for other ways to evaluate your training.

Remember that your learners will gain much from a program that is well planned, involves them in decisions about their learning, and has a logical flow. Evaluation is essential to keep your program effective. The next chapter will help you design instruction that is engaging and challenging for your adult learners.

## Worksheet 2-5. Other Ways to Measure Results

**Written Responses**

☐ Individual Test or Quiz

☐ Group Test or Quiz

☐ Essay

☐ Other_____

**Demonstration**

☐ Individuals must successfully complete a task, demonstrating their new skill

☐ Individuals must present (this can be a live or recorded presentation)

☐ Individuals or groups must teach others what they have successfully learned

☐ Other _____

**Verbal Responses**

☐ Individual or group interviews by the instructor

☐ Fishbowl (evaluators or other participants look and listen in on a discussion to identify appropriate or inappropriate answers)

☐ Participants dramatize new learning—these could be live or recorded

☐ Other _____

**Role Playing**

☐ Participants pretend to be subjects for other participants who demonstrate their new knowledge or skills

☐ Put on a drama that illustrates the new learning

☐ Simulations that depict what participants need to know and do

☐ Other_____

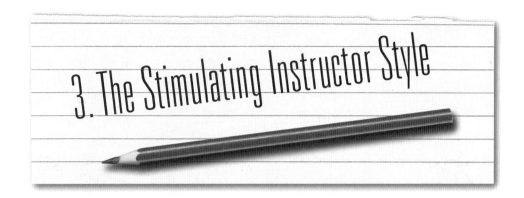

# 3. The Stimulating Instructor Style

Adults become motivated to learn when they are challenged with new ideas that are presented in interesting and lively ways. The stimulating instructor style is characterized by provocative presentations that inspire and persuade learners to change their attitudes and behavior. Information is presented in ways that engage participants and make them think. The stimulating strategies and learning tactics in this chapter will help you design instruction that is interesting, dynamic, and makes an impact on your participants. When instruction is stimulating, lasting positive change is possible.

Stimulating strategies include the following:

- Present information in interesting and useful ways.
- Use active learning approaches.
- Encourage creativity.
- Help learners solve real problems.
- Help participants practice new learning.

## 💡 Stimulating Strategy 6: Present Information in Interesting and Useful Ways

Adults tend to think and act in familiar and rigid patterns. Instructors must cause adults to change by challenging the old and introducing the new as a valid alternative.

Though lectures can be deadly, instructors commonly use this teaching method to get their ideas across. Lectures are quick and easy. They are *efficient* at getting a message across but may not be the most *effective*. That is, they may not accomplish your goal, which is to create positive sustainable change in your participants. Lectures may be effective under certain conditions:

- The topic is vitally important to the audience. For example, if you are on board a sinking ship and the captain is explaining the best method for getting on the lifeboats, you will very likely pay close attention and follow his instructions.

- The lecturer is so admired or loved that you pay attention out of loyalty and pure devotion. If Elvis returned and spoke to his fans, they would hang on his every word.

- The speaker is so highly charismatic and forceful that the listeners become magically absorbed in wonder and awe. This is rare but we have all heard such speakers and we are moved and even transformed in those moments. Combine those three elements and you have one powerful lecture.

Now consider the average adult instructor. We are called upon to teach in our company meeting rooms, college classes, churches, or community organizations. Calculate the degree to which we are afforded honor and loyalty and…well, let's face it, we need to do more than just stand up and lecture to make a significant impact or effect meaningful change. Even if you are not a celebrity or even particularly charismatic, you can still present your good ideas to participants in ways that will be effective.

The following tactics reinforce the stimulating instructor style.

## Tactic 6.1: The "Lecturette" – A Very Short Lecture

**Purpose:** Presents information in a format that is brief and easy to digest.

**Description:** The lecturette is a short talk that presents the main points or principles to a group. Some key points in using the lecturette:

- Conciseness: Make it short—from one to 15 minutes.

- Precision: Provide only the essential information needed to move a group forward.

- Illumination: Offer information that is unique and new to the audience, provides a different twist, or sheds new light on the subject.

- Illustration: The lecturette should be accompanied by demonstrations, stories, or visual aids to help you show as well as tell.

- Context: The lecturette should fit neatly into one's total presentation. It can be used to introduce or summarize some activity. You can use lecturettes in a series that build on each other to a grand conclusion.

## Tactic 6.2: Sequencing

**Purpose:** Provides a logical pattern for presenting training content, resulting in better understanding and retention.

**Description:** Pay attention to how you organize your ideas depending on the subject matter and your target audience. Here are some options for organizing your presentations:

- Option 1: Opening, Middle, Closing. Lectures or speeches often have this pattern. Begin with an attention-getting opening such as a question, startling set of facts, or a challenge. The middle part of your presentation should answer the question or respond to the facts or challenge. The end summarizes the main point or conclusion.

- Option 2: General to Specific. You can organize a talk or a whole curriculum with this pattern. Begin with a general concept and narrow it down to small details.

- Option 3: Simple to Complex. Begin with the simplest concepts and move on to more complicated concepts. If you were to teach active listening, you might start with simple skills like eye contact and posture for better listening. Then move on to more advanced skills such as paraphrasing and summarizing. The next level of complexity is teaching skills that are more akin to counseling and consulting.

- Option 4: The List. Sometimes ideas are organized in a simple list. For example, in this very chapter we have created lists of learning tactics. The instructor just goes down a list (using no special order) describing and demonstrating each one in turn. Adding handouts and using visuals to this type of presentation results in better learning retention.

- Option 5: Problem Solving. Start with problem definition (where we are), next move on to the desired outcomes (where we want to be), and finally lay out the solutions (how to get where we want to be).

- Option 6: Logic Pyramid. Start by presenting your main points; offer supporting evidence for each point in turn, and then end with a conclusion. This structure is effective when trying to persuade as well as teach an audience.

## Tactic 6.3: Visual Aids

**Purpose:** Visual aids add punch to your teaching points.

**Description:** Your ideas will stick longer when you add visual reinforcement as you teach. Worksheet 3-1 provides a checklist of ideas for visual aids.

## Tactic 6.4: Readings

**Purpose:** Presents information or directions in written form.

**Description:** Have you ever thought it would be better to be handed something to read rather than listen to a talk? If you provide handouts that cover the same material you plan to talk about, why not just let participants read it for themselves? Print material in manageable chunks (list of important points or distinct paragraphs). This lets participants absorb the information, discuss it in small groups, and then solicit questions from individuals in the larger group.

### Worksheet 3-1. Visual Aid Idea Checklist

- ☐ Blackboard or whiteboard
- ☐ Books
- ☐ Buttons and badges
- ☐ Constructions
- ☐ Costumes
- ☐ Decorations relevant to your theme
- ☐ Demonstrations
- ☐ Displays
- ☐ Drawings
- ☐ Flipchart
- ☐ Flowcharts (on paper, charts, on the floor, walls, or ceiling)
- ☐ Handouts
- ☐ Object lessons
- ☐ Overhead projections (slides, transparencies, laptop computer presentations)
- ☐ Photographs
- ☐ Physical objects as metaphors (a glass half full or is it half empty?)
- ☐ Posters
- ☐ Show-and-tell
- ☐ Skits
- ☐ Sticky notes
- ☐ Video conferencing
- ☐ Videos
- ☐ Wall hangings
- ☐ Your ideas _____

## Tactic 6.5: Demonstrations

**Purpose:** Provides a lesson through demonstrated actions.

**Description:** A demonstration is a powerful way to teach because it offers a way to learn by seeing and hearing. If people can hear, see, touch, and ask questions they will retain information better. In a listening workshop, the instructor demonstrates the skills needed for good listening before learners try it. For adults, a demonstration is an advanced form of the show-and-tell we recall from our preschool days. It works just as well with adults as it does with kids.

## Tactic 6.6: Learners as Teachers

**Purpose:** Teaches the teacher as well as the learner.

**Description:** The task of acquiring knowledge or skills can be divided into steps or separate units that individuals or groups of learners can master. Each person or group becomes an "expert" on this particular subtopic and then they teach it to other learners. Here are some ways to get your learners teaching each other:

- Assign the task of teaching a portion of your lesson to individuals who volunteer.
- Put portions of the content into the hands of a small group. They master the material and then check in with you before teaching it to others.
- "Team-teach" a topic with participant volunteers.
- Create teams whose task it is to share what they learn with each other and answer each other's questions. The instructor becomes a consultant to the teams.
- Discover who in your workshop or class is already familiar with portions of the topic or possesses to some extent the skills being taught, and let them teach.
- Facilitate a learning exchange where each small group teaches another small group or they take turns teaching the larger group.

## Tactic 6.7: Speaking Tips

**Purpose:** Encourages effective speaking.

**Description:** Listed below are some important tips for effective speaking. (There are some great books and websites available to help you develop effective speaking skills. Two of our favorites are *Fearless Public Speaking With Steve Pool* by Steve Pool, and a blog that covers presentation skills and speechwriting, "Six Minutes Speaking and Presentation Skills," at www.sixminutes.dlugan.com.)

- Remind yourself constantly that your audience, not you, matters most.
- Be yourself—but be your best you.

- Conserve words—don't ramble.

- Use good posture, eye contact, and gesture as you focus on your audience.

- Speak more slowly than seems natural and project your voice. Talk to the back of the room.

- Use discreet notes or note cards and make sure to keep them in order.

- Use visuals (best not to overload a PowerPoint presentation with wordiness).

- Use appropriate voice inflections and well-planned pauses.

- Overcome nervousness—use deep breathing or other techniques to overcome nervousness; wear comfortable clothing that will not show perspiration; minimize hand movements if you are shaky; remind yourself that you have an important message for your audience that they will appreciate.

- Practice—perfect your timing, sequence, stories, and use of visual aids.

- Rehearse in front of an imaginary audience, a mirror, or some good friends.

Also see chapter 7 for the Sample Workshop: "Impress for Success—Learning How to Deliver Effective Presentations."

#  Stimulating Strategy 7: Use Active Learning Approaches

Experienced instructors know that adults learn by doing, not just sitting and hearing someone talk at them. Variety is the spice of life *and* learning. Adults should be actively involved in learning tasks at least 50 percent of the time. Use various methods that engage your learners' emotions, critical thinking, and multiple senses (hearing, seeing, touching, or doing). Informational presentations should always be balanced with experiential learning activities.

## Two Instructional Modes

Here is a model for ensuring your instruction involves active learning. This model involves two instructional approaches—*action to analysis* and *analysis to action.*

The *action-to-analysis* mode involves an activity that stimulates critical thinking and allows learners to discover and discuss important principles from the activity. For example, participants are asked to cross their arms the way they do it naturally. Then they are asked to cross their arms the "other" way—opposite of the "natural" way. This is the action. Next, they are asked, "What would it take for you to change so you always crossed your arms the 'other' (less natural) way?" Their responses are listed on a flipchart and discussed. The instructor can follow this up with a lecturette on current research about change and growth in adults. This is the analysis. You will be pleased to find that adult participants will virtually teach themselves in these situations—you simply become a facilitator in the process. You can reverse the process by having students first read or hear about the concept and then try the experiment.

Lynn offers this example of action to analysis when teaching adults to deliver more effective presentations: Demonstrate the distracting behaviors some presenters display, such as twirling of the hair, jangling change in a pants pocket, using fillers such as "ya know" or "um." Ask the participants to take note of anything they see that distracts them from the message. This is the action. Next, listen to what they found distracting, record their answers on a flipchart, and discuss how to overcome these distractions.

In the *analysis-to-action* mode, the instructor presents some key ideas and then asks the group to try them out. For example, in a listening workshop participants are taught the principles and skills of good listening. This is the analysis. After questions are answered and participants are clear on what is expected, they participate in practice sessions, where observers, listeners, and talkers rotate roles and hone their listening skills. They apply what they learned. This is the action. You can reverse the process by having students listen to each other and then ask: What worked best?

Instructors can also use both instructional modes. For example, after explaining how to listen actively and asking participants to practice the skills (analysis to action) the instructor could ask participants to list some insights and discoveries they made during the practice (action to analysis). This deepens and reinforces the learning. In Table 3-1, the roles of the instructor and participants in this model are presented.

The following tactics reinforce the stimulating instructor style.

## Tactic 7.1: Movement

**Purpose:** Keeps learning lively.

**Description:** Get people moving around in the learning space. At first, adults are very reluctant to get up and move around. Adults have been conditioned to sit still and listen. Assign participants to gather themselves in small groups or pairs. Insist that small groups sit close enough so neighboring small groups will not interfere with each other's work.

In a class on networking, learners were instructed to bring 10 business cards or write their names and contact information on 10 index cards. They were to note their talents or offerings and their potential needs. Next they walked around the room and talked to as many people as they could, and when they found a match of an offering and a need, they exchanged information. The room buzzed and the trainer had difficulty drawing the group back together for the remainder of the instruction.

You can send small groups to cluster in corners to complete assignments. Label the corners and have people cluster under the appropriate labels, then change the labels and have them rearrange themselves according to the new categories. Remember that adults will initially balk at moving around. However, when the class is over adults will thank you for getting them moving.

## Table 3-1. Instructional Modes: Instructor and Learner Roles

| ANALYSIS ⟶ | ACTION |
|---|---|
| Instructor: teaches, demonstrates, illustrates, or elicits from the students the key principles, knowledge, or skills that need to be learned. This can include helping the students find learning resources that teach the basic ideas. | Instructor: creates experiences, organizes field trips, gives instructions, sets up experiments, encourages, guides, and critiques students as they make discoveries about what they learned from the analysis. |
| Learner: listens, watches, reads, takes notes, absorbs, contributes ideas, thinks, analyzes, imagines, and so on. | Learner: practices, follows directions, experiments, tries out, rehearses, plays with, takes risks, discovers, and so on. |
| **ACTION ⟶** | **ANALYSIS** |
| Instructor: creates experiences, designs activities, provides tools, and gives instructions for exploration. The activities should be designed so they naturally lead the learners toward discoveries. | Instructor: facilitates discussion, draws out truths from the actions observed or experienced. The teacher helps the learners make sense out of the action by collating information or helping them draw conclusions. |
| Learner: explores, manipulates, gets involved, tries things out, immerses self in tasks, takes risks, follows directions, stays alert to new learning, and so on. | Learner: thinks about principles, compares, draws conclusions, makes lists, writes papers, and so on. |

## Tactic 7.2: Debate

**Purpose:** Helps learners gain knowledge through active persuasion.

**Description:** People disagree when participating in learning experiences. Why not formalize it and stage a debate on some of the more controversial topics? Choose a topic and let learners line up on one side or another. The side a person takes is not as important as being able to use newly-learned information gained in the process of debating. What will make your case most effective? What facts do you need? What opinions are being present-ed? What is the basic premise? Learners can caucus with their supportive group, formulate their plan, and then challenge the opposing team.

## Tactic 7.3: Participant Demonstrations

**Purpose:** Involves learners by making them responsible for an activity.

**Description:** Participants can make posters, put on skits, and create displays to demon-strate new learning. Have props ready for individuals or groups to use. If you teach a skill, you will find demonstrations invaluable. A good pattern to follow: Tell them how, show them how, and then let them demonstrate. Follow this up with a debriefing session.

## Tactic 7.4: Case Studies or Scenarios

**Purpose:** Teaches by working on sample problems.

**Description:** This is a classic way to engage learners. Written scenarios or case studies help learners begin to understand and manipulate the real world safely. First, show photos or video of a marketing campaign. You can create a fictional or real example about a manager who had to handle a difficult behavioral situation and let the participants work on a solu-tion. The groups discuss and critique it and then report their findings and suggestions for improvement. Another approach is to first teach a method for handling certain situations. Next, ask learners to use the new method in a case study.

## Tactic 7.5: Drama and Role Play

**Purpose:** Teaches through dramatic simulations.

**Description:** Drama is fun for some, not for others. Those who like drama should be allowed to express themselves. Dramas need audiences so do not force everyone to be actors. People can be live props or help with setting the scene.

Role playing can take place among two or three learners without having to face an audience. Set the scene, specify the behaviors you want dramatized, and then let small groups work on their own. The instructor can wander around the room and act as a consultant. Some groups may volunteer to put on their role play for others, but it is not necessary that they do so.

## Tactic 7.6: Small Groups and Inter-Group Sharing

**Purpose:** Uses dialogue to teach.

**Description:** Give a small group of adults an interesting topic to discuss and they will quickly get involved. When individuals in a small group wrestle with ideas and concepts, they learn from each other. You can follow this up with small groups reporting their discoveries. Mix and match groups. Have them discuss a topic or work on a problem and then reverse the process.

#  Stimulating Strategy 8: Encourage Creativity

Adults should be engaged in creating and experimenting with new knowledge to foster change and growth. Help them invent, originate, conceive, author, and express their creative side by removing fear and ambivalence. Present a process that helps adults take a creative risk.

Instructors can help adults become creative by providing a framework in which they feel free to explore options. A group of supervisors will find it easier to think of ways to better manage their workgroups if they are given categories to guide their creative thinking. For example, they might be asked to think of ways that will help their employees learn new skills or policies, how to solve problems, how to form project teams, and so forth. The participants, armed with a list of categories as a guide, come up with their own ideas. In other words, the instructor provides the categories and the participants provide the originality and creative thinking.

Creativity is the active use of imagination to produce something unique. It goes beyond painting a picture or composing music. It means drawing on your inner resources to produce a new thought or point of view, an artistic representation, an idea, or solution to a problem. We all have an urge to create in some form or another. As adults, we tend to be creatures of habit and routine, but we are all quite capable of exploring, inventing, and improving our world. Adult learners need to affirm their own creative powers in problem solving and artistic expression.

When we learn, we reinvent ourselves—our behavior, knowledge, and understanding. The very act of learning, therefore, is creative. Adult instructors have a unique opportunity to facilitate the process of creative transformation in our participants. Allowing adults to invent, originate, conceive, author, and imagine aids in learning, change, and growth. The relationship between creativity and learning is summarized in Table 3-2.

The following tactics reinforce the stimulating instructor style.

## Tactic 8.1: Remembering

**Purpose:** Helps adults recall their creative moments.

**Description:** Provide a definition of creativity such as this: "Being creative means drawing on your inner resources or your imagination to bring about something new. This can result in a pleasing photograph, work of art, a unique solution to a problem, or an idea that makes others stop and rethink what they are doing." Based on this definition, ask participants to recall one or two incidents when they were creative as children, youth, or as adults. (Instructors may want to share some examples from their own creative past.) Have them think of what conditions surrounded those incidents. Next, participants should share with a partner or small group. Collect these moments on a flipchart and see what the group discovers about their patterns of creativity. Most people have forgotten some wonderful examples of being creative. As you ask this group to be creative in your session, you will have plenty of evidence to encourage them.

### Table 3-2. How the Creative Process Aids Learning

| While engaging in creative thinking, adults become more: | Because creativity... |
|---|---|
| Involved | ...draws one fully into an activity. |
| Wakeful | ...calls for complete attention. |
| Energized | ...makes one feel alive. |
| Aware | ...heightens one's sensitivity. |
| Flexible | ...causes one to drop old ways of doing things. |
| Positive | ...is hopeful and friendly. |
| Focused | ...calls for sustained attention. |
| Daring | ...calls one to adventure and to take risks. |
| Delighted | ...is enjoyable. |
| Childlike | ...makes one feel young. |
| Reachable | ...opens one up to new experiences and ideas. |
| Inventive | ...causes one to make new connections. |

## Tactic 8.2: Provide Tools for Creativity

**Purpose:** Gives learners what they need to be creative.

**Description:** A tool is simply a means to an end. More precisely, tools are the necessary materials, instructions, techniques, or instruments needed to perform some task, in this case to create something. If you are going to facilitate creativity you must carefully think through and provide all the tools necessary for the task. For example:

- clear instructions for your participants
- enough supplies for everyone

- backing material—paper, poster board

- adhesives—tape, glue

- media—paint, pencils, clay

- miscellaneous—paper, magazines, beads, string

- sufficient space for working—table surfaces, floor space

- surfaces—protective coating

- scripts—scenarios, role descriptions

- resources—reference books, song books, idea stimulators.

## Tactic 8.3: Provide a Clear Example

**Purpose:** Helps learners get started with an example to guide them.

**Description:** When adults are first challenged to be inventive and creative it helps to give some examples of what you are looking for. This might be called a *vision of quality*. If you ask learners to write a cooperative group poem, read one of yours or provide samples from other groups. If you ask for an idea to be presented as a collage, have one prepared to show. Because adults tend to rely on replicating your example instead of stretching themselves to achieve something truly novel, emphasize that all the learner's work must be completely original. Once a work is done, however, never criticize learners' attempts at creativity—remember that creativity cannot be forced.

## Tactic 8.4: Set Clear Boundaries

**Purpose:** Promotes freedom by setting limits.

**Description:** Paradoxically, boundaries help us feel free—this is strange but true. The canvas for the artist sets a parameter. The lump of clay, just so big, limits the potter. When you ask participants to generate new ideas it is helpful to suggest limits. ("Think of three ways to improve input from employees," or "You have three minutes to come up with a new plan.") Besides providing boundaries, setting limits allows participants to focus their efforts and adds to the fun.

Some ways instructors set boundaries to encourage creativity include:

- Time limits—"Your group has just 10 minutes to work."

- Space limits—"Use only what you find in this room to create a role play."

- Subject or topic limits—"Groups one and two are to think of ways to prevent these problems and groups three and four are to think of ways to solve them."

- Thematic limits—"Create a poem about a time-management problem."

- Limit the size of work group—"Get into groups of three and…"

- Simplify the task—"Create a song using the tune of…"

- Limit the number of responses—"Think of five ideas to improve this process."

- Limit the number of steps in a process: "One, state that you are uncomfortable about a conflict. Two, state why you are uncomfortable. Three, find a compromise. Four, come to an agreement."

- Limit the purpose—"Think of some ways to help a new employee feel confident about his responsibilities."

## Tactic 8.5: Encourage the Creative Risk

**Purpose:** Helps adults overcome fears of failure when being creative.

**Description:** The fear of failure that adults associate with being creative is often based on past experiences. Fear of ridicule can be a powerful deterrent to creative efforts. This fear looms large particularly when learners are asked to share their efforts with others. The most effective way to encourage learners is to assure them that failure is not possible and ridicule will not occur. The least effective way is to try to push or persuade adults to perform, especially in front of others.

Set the tone for creativity with these assurances:

- The goal of the activity is to aid in learning something, not to perform wonders. This is not a test of their creative potential. It is only a means to an end.

- Creativity is a process, not a product. It is a process of generation-reaction-re-generation. It is not a once-and-for-all event.

- There are no "wrong answers" in a creative exercise. A vision of quality is not a measure of success. It is simply a launching pad for the creative process.

- You will not judge participants and others should follow your model of acceptance and respect for everyone's efforts. In learning, there is a time for evaluation, but the time for creativity should be judgment-free.

- A learning environment is a place to experiment, a place for uncertainty.

- Promote the idea that participants and instructors form a learning community, which is characterized by mutual support. Effective learning takes place as we work together to gain skill, knowledge, and understanding.

## Tactic 8.6: Share and Celebrate Creativity

**Purpose:** Reinforces creative efforts.

**Description:** When adult learners stretch themselves to be creative, it deserves some recognition. Create opportunities to share the results with others and celebrate. This can be simple or elaborate depending on the circumstance.

Here are some ideas for sharing and celebrating:

- Ask a person from each group of participants to report to the whole class.
- Have small groups take turns showing or demonstrating their creative work.
- Help each group to set up a station and ask groups to rotate to view them all.
- Suggest that each individual show and tell a subgroup or the whole class.
- Ask each group to pass its work around the room for appreciation.
- Make a video presentation for all to watch.
- Create a display encompassing the whole class's effort for outsiders.
- Publish a class paper using participant work.
- Create a photo display.
- Encourage the whole class to cheer and applaud heartily after group or individual reports are made.
- Give a prize to all participants or for certain qualities of a presentation (most lively, colorful, daring, ambitious, and so forth).
- Have a party!
- Applaud *all* efforts.

## Tactic 8.7: Four Phases of Creativity

**Purpose:** Uses a process to enhance creativity.

**Description:** One way of thinking about creativity is in these four phases: reflect, release, receive, and respond. You can prepare learners for creative activities by allowing time for them to go through each creative phase.

- Reflect: Reflection involves relaxation, quieting the mind, centering the mind, and becoming silent to allow the creative thought process to begin. Some methods for reflection include deep breathing, meditation, guided imagery, journaling, and quiet conversation.
- Release: This step involves letting go of distractions such as worries and cares and day-to-day concerns. This is the time to free oneself from prescribed methods and past patterns and liberate the mind to see things in new ways.

Some methods include writing, mentally letting all thoughts go, and a physical motion such as releasing something with palms down.

- Receive: Now is the time to allow new ideas to flow in. This step involves free-associating, exploring, sorting, choosing, and structuring thoughts and ideas. This is the nitty-gritty process of discovering the novel idea or fresh viewpoint. Some methods include brainstorming, listing, free-associating, experimenting, discussing, mind mapping, questioning, trying out words, storytelling, and testing.

- Respond: This is when the ideas are expressed. Now is the time to make the decision, sling the paint, or sing the song. Try out the new solution, either in simulation or under real conditions. Some methods include creating a work of art, writing, and performing.

##  Stimulating Strategy 9: Help Learners Solve Real Problems

Adults should be engaged in solving important and relevant problems. Problem-solving techniques can be taught and used to reinforce the course content. Encourage learners to work on decisions or issues that they face in their daily lives.

We've found that learners are motivated when they are solving problems that are important to them. In a new employee orientation class, invite motivated and effective current employees to speak about the problems and possibilities the new hires will face in their new jobs. The learners will see the procedural information they then get from the trainers in a new light. ("I can apply this to my situation.")

When learners are engaged in solving problems they actively think and apply the new understanding, knowledge, and skills they are learning. This kind of engagement increases the effectiveness and enjoyment of learning.

The following tactics reinforce the stimulating instructor style.

### Tactic 9.1: Active Listening

**Purpose:** Uses active listening to learn about and solve problems.

**Description:** You can use this method with learners grouped in threes or in pairs. In a group of three, you will have a listener, speaker, and observer with rotating roles. The speaker shares a problem while the listener uses active listening skills. As the listener listens and facilitates the speaker's reflections, solutions begin to emerge. Finally, the observer joins the conversation and the group attempts to articulate a final and best solution.

Often you may find that just being listened to causes the speaker to find solutions as she shares a problem. This is a key element of counseling or psychotherapy. A good listener, even a nonprofessional counselor, can be a catalyst for insight and change by the speaker.

This process works well with partners, too. The listener and speaker both take turns in each role. The listener takes notes, which are shared with the speaker, and they discuss the problem as they commonly understand it, and then explore and decide upon a solution.

## Tactic 9.2: Participant Consultants

**Purpose:** Teaches by facilitating a solution.

**Description:** After presenting a topic or skill, the instructor divides the class into "clients" and "consultants." The instructor presents case problems to the clients (or participants use real problems they face) and the consultants assist them in working toward solutions based on the lesson content. Next, the clients and consultants switch roles and receive new problems to solve. The instructor may want to devise some special instructions for the consultants or provide a guide sheet for both roles to follow.

Here is a sample consultation instruction: Listen to your partner as you ask the following guiding queries.

- What is the concern you have?
- How would you like things to be?
- What obstacles are there?
- What ways can you think of to achieve your goal?
- What is your plan?
- What is your first step?

## Tactic 9.3: Like-Minded Meetings

**Purpose:** To enable problem solving as people with similar interests join forces.

**Description:** The instructor asks learners who have a special interest in a problem to work together. For example, in an instructor training workshop, groups of learners work on solutions to problems such as how to manage difficult participants, or how to navigate mandated training sessions. The small groups report their solutions to the larger group. A variation on this is to have people who are unaffected by the problem work on the solution, as they can provide fresh, unbiased perspectives.

## Tactic 9.4: Problem-Solving Teams

**Purpose:** Provides long-term problem solving through team effort.

**Description:** The problem-solving team is a group that stays together and works on a particular problem over an extended period. This may be an all-day team in a workshop or collaboration among participants outside of the workshop who come back together after a period of time to report results. The team studies the problem in-depth and then makes periodic reports or a final report.

### Tactic 9.5: Help Exchange

**Purpose:** Encourages learners to share problems and find quick solutions.

**Description:** Individuals or small groups write out specific problems they want help with and then the problems are passed from group to group with solutions added to the paper as it progresses. The originator receives the list of solutions at the end of the round. Originators of each problem can discuss the range of solutions and select the best ones to try out.

### Tactic 9.6: Symbolic or Simulated Problem Solving

**Purpose:** Uses simulations and games to solve problems.

**Description:** Real problems can be simulated allowing participants to apply new knowledge and skills:

- Acted-out scenarios—actors portray problem situations for participants to solve. The action starts and people can join in the skit with their solutions.

- Case studies—present common problems in written form, recordings, or videos.

- Puzzles—use puzzles to simulate real problems (redesign board games and puzzles to fit your topic, or create riddles that allow participants to use their new knowledge and skills)

- Electronic simulations

- Play it again—participants describe a scenario that they participated in that could have been better handled. Actors play it as described, followed by a group discussion, then they play it again as it might have been.

### Tactic 9.7: Circle of Advice

**Purpose:** Helps learners share answers with the whole group.

**Description:** Volunteers or students with special qualifications sit in an inner circle. The rest of the learners sit around the outside looking in and listening. Problems are brought before this group of "experts" and they take turns presenting solutions or they may choose to pass. They may also discuss among themselves. Follow this with small group discussions on what was learned or a general summary presented to the whole group.

# Stimulating Strategy 10: Help Participants Practice New Knowledge and Skills

Learners should be able to practice applying what they've learned and receive feedback. They need an opportunity to rehearse actions they may be called upon to perform in the future in real work scenarios. This strategy is similar to the rehearsal for an actor. The goal of rehearsal is to be prepared when the curtain goes up, just as participants need to be prepared for roles in life and work.

Learning should be like entering a refuge or shelter where one is free to make mistakes. You are gently guided into becoming more proficient, competent, knowledgeable, or wise. In a learning role, you are protected. Nevertheless, this refuge must prepare you for the real world. After learners have spent time learning, they will return to their normal work or personal life situations where they will be called upon to apply what they've learned. However, even if just for an hour, the workshop or class should be a safe haven in which learners can prepare to face the responsibility to come.

The following tactics reinforce the stimulating instructor style.

## Tactic 10.1: Plan, Write, and Review

**Purpose:** Provides conceptual practice.

**Description:** After teaching concepts, ask learners to make specific plans that describe how they will apply the new ideas in their lives or work roles. Learners write out these plans and then share them with a partner, small group, or the whole class for review and critique. The written record is a valuable takeaway for guiding future performance.

## Tactic 10.2: Demonstrate Using Skill Standards

**Purpose:** Uses standards to guide practice.

**Description:** Learners may want and need to be able to demonstrate very specific levels of ability in order to ensure learning has been mastered. Some ways to set up this practice include:

- The instructor can observe learners and assess their performance.
- Learners can be trained to assess each other's performance.
- Small groups can practice until each member reaches a desired level of performance.
- A panel of judges made up of learners or experts can be used for assessments that are more subjective.

## Tactic 10.3: Video Feedback

**Purpose:** Use immediate video feedback to objectify practice.

**Description:** Being observed with a camera so you can see your mistakes and successes adds potency to the experience. Seeing ourselves as others see us brings an element of reality to practice. Sitting down with a mentor or coach to look at the video helps learners hone skills. A series of video sessions is better than a single exposure. Schedule these knowing that this process can be very time consuming. (See chapter 7 for further discussion of this method.)

## Tactic 10.4: Practitioner/Expert Review

**Purpose:** Use experienced practitioners to assist with rehearsal.

**Description:** Send learners out to practitioners or bring practitioners into the classroom to review learner practice sessions. An effective way to practice good supervisory skills is to do so in the company of those who already have the skills and can critique the learner. Many practitioners are willing and eager to do this as a service to their field.

## Tactic 10.5: Field Work/Intern(extern)-ships

**Purpose:** Provides on-the-job training.

**Description:** This has been a classic way of providing practice in many fields. Participants are asked to do the real job assisted by a mentor, or under observation, in a setting where the work really takes place. It is important to remember for classroom or field instructors that the primary goal of an internship is instruction and not production.

## Tactic 10.6: Small Group of Peers

**Purpose:** Provides safety in numbers when practicing.

**Description:** Using learning teams or small, temporary support groups can ease the tension while practicing. The goal for these small groups is to help each member become as knowledgeable and proficient as possible. An element of friendly competition can be added to increase the fun and motivation. When the group feels that each member is ready, they demonstrate for the whole class.

## Tactic 10.7: Rehearsal or Role Play

**Purpose:** Simulates real life.

**Description:** Role playing should be used with great care. Many adults are reluctant to act in front of a large group. It is best to use role play in small groups. Always allow adult participants an opportunity to pass. Here is a suggested method:

1. Clearly define the skills learners will practice.

2. Demonstrate the skills you want learners to practice.

3. Divide participants into the smallest group units possible.

4. Allow small groups to select roles, practice, and assess their own members.

5. Act as a roving consultant and facilitator.

# 4. The Spontaneous Instructor Style

Spontaneous instruction gives adults the opportunity and permission to try out new ways of learning and to break free from old patterns. Unpredictability fosters the process of "unfreezing" adults from the same old line of thinking. Plan and allow for play, humor, and surprise in your instruction. When adults play, laugh, and take risks together, resistance to new ideas and information tends to weaken and fall. This chapter presents strategies and learning tactics that will help you liberate your learners from conventional ways of understanding and behaving. When instruction is spontaneous, anything can happen, which not only frees the learners but the instructor as well.

Spontaneous strategies include the following:

- Help learners tell their stories.
- Make it funny, make it fun.
- Use imagination and the arts.
- Build in risk taking.
- Take time to reflect.

##  Spontaneous Strategy 11: Help Learners Tell Their Stories

Adults like to hear and tell stories. Much learning can take place as adults share their personal stories and experiences, because they often contain practical solutions to work-related problems. The instructor should structure the session so that a significant portion of the course content flows from these interactions.

Form small groups when you use this strategy because a smaller audience often allows adults to tell their stories more comfortably. Once you get them started, it is difficult to get them to stop. Telling stories is an ancient means of passing on wisdom: "How did you solve the problem I now face?" and "Where did you find a resource?" In fact, adults often come to training sessions just to meet and talk with others who face similar situations.

The reason this strategy fits with the spontaneous style is that it adds a measure of unpredictability to instruction. Instructors may guide and direct these exchanges, hoping they result in significant insight, learning, and change, but we cannot fully know the extent to which they actually will.

The following tactics help unearth learner's personal experiences.

## Tactic 11.1: Small Groups

**Purpose:** Facilitates participant storytelling through the use of small groups.

**Description:** The ideal group size is a matter of debate among facilitators. The best size for close, intimate interaction is three members in a group. The maximum size for discussion groups should be five or six, depending on the task and time frame. A group of three allows all learners to take part in the discussion. When the group size exceeds six, some members of the group will begin to exert more control and others will start to fade into the background.

## Tactic 11.2: Extended Group Projects

**Purpose:** Stresses the value of groups staying together to achieve a common goal.

**Description:** Small groups are powerful units for learning. To make them more effective, keep small groups meeting together over an extended period rather than frequently dissolving and rearranging groups. Trust created through interaction over longer periods of time provides a greater opportunity for mutual teaching and learning. This emotional closeness combined with mutual work usually results in positive learning.

## Tactic 11.3: Seating Arrangements

**Purpose:** Promotes physical closeness that helps members interact more freely.

**Description:** When you begin small group activities, ask participants to get into a small circle and try to "touch knees." This physical closeness may meet with some resistance so use good judgment, but communicate the importance of direct, close interaction. Point out that being close reduces the interference from conversation in other groups nearby.

Do your best to prevent groups from sitting in a line; in this formation, people on the ends are left out and mentally drift away. Having flexible seating helps, but you can create good personal connections in large auditoriums with more rigid seating if participants turn toward people behind them or move to open spaces for conversation or activity.

## Tactic 11.4: Use Learners' Life Experiences

**Purpose:** Promotes the value of adult learners' life experience and knowledge.

**Description:** Instructors are wise to acknowledge the great wealth of knowledge, expertise, and wisdom of learners. Even if we unwisely decide we want only our ideas expressed, adult learners filter it through their own past experience anyway and reject what does not fit. Here are some reasons to use the prior knowledge and skill of the learners in the teaching process.

- Tried and true. Learner knowledge and skills are valuable because they are learned through prior experience. Often their ideas have been tried and proven to be accurate and effective.

- Reinforces the instructor's points. Even if information from learners is not quite accurate, the instructor can correct their input and guide learners to draw valuable inferences from each other's stories that reinforce key points in the lesson.

- Adds variety and depth. The comments of other learners are often a welcome relief after spending so much time listening to just one person's point of view.

- Helps everyone enjoy the learning more. The exchange of ideas is fun and profitable. Even a good argument sharpens our reasoning and leaves us tingling and energized.

- Adds a greater sense of ownership by the learners. Empowered learners are better learners.

- Increases effectiveness and efficiency of instruction. When we delegate, collaborate, and cooperate we get more for the energy expended.

- Peer opinions are credible. The opinions of one's peers often seem more credible than even those of the instructor. The smart instructor uses the power of peer influence for the good of learning.

Here are some structured ways to use learners' life experiences and wisdom to further learning:

- Know your group. Assess the knowledge and experience of the learners by inquiring about what they know and do not know about the topic—you can use an in-class survey, pretest, or a verbal inquiry to accomplish this.

- Form small groups. Small discussion or work groups provide an opportunity for learners to share their wisdom.

- Let learners present. Formal or informal presentations by learners, when they are given adequate time to prepare, will enrich the group's experience. You can either stand aside or facilitate these moments.

- Let learners demonstrate. Demonstrations by learners that support class content can add considerable depth to the learning experience. A demonstration is an adult version of show-and-tell and is an effective way to show practical applications of the content.

- Learners can become consultants or mentors to each other. This takes careful matching of those with expertise to those who need guidance.

- More experienced and advanced participants can tutor those who are struggling. Tutors can be assigned or volunteer to help. Tutoring can be offered when requested by anyone in the class or everyone can take turns being a tutor.

- Learners can help answer their peers' questions. An easy and effective way to glean the wisdom from a group is to turn questions, directed toward instructors, back to the group. When a participant asks a question you can defer to the class: "Does anyone have an answer to this?"

## Tactic 11.5: Reaction Groups

**Purpose:** Allows learners to systematically respond to content.

**Description:** After a presentation, you can ask participants to form reaction groups to respond to it. These can meet for just a few minutes or for a longer time. After reactions are discussed, let anyone share what they discovered. You can appoint or ask for volunteers to form a participant review panel. Each person can speak and then the audience can respond or ask questions.

## Tactic 11.6: Guided Interaction

**Purpose:** Structures interaction to facilitate storytelling.

**Description:** You may want to structure learner interactions to encourage storytelling among them. Sentence completions are a good way to do that. Read a sentence and then ask each person in turn to finish the sentence. Some examples: *When I first enter a new group I feel… In my opinion an effective supervisor is one who… The best boss I ever had…* and so forth.

Another way to get learners to share stories is to introduce a topic and ask individuals in small groups to share any story they know about the topic. Topics might include a good marketing plan, a good listener, best team effort, and so forth. Good stories can be shared with the whole audience.

# Spontaneous Strategy 12: Make It Funny, Make It Fun

Opportunities for playfulness encourage adults to laugh and enjoy themselves while learning. Use and promote humor that facilitates learning, is in good taste, supports the content, and matches participant values. Encourage surprise, serendipity, and fun in the learning encounter.

Some principles for using humor in teaching adults:

- Never use humor that might ridicule any person, group, or culture. A good test is to imagine telling it to people who are the object of humor or a joke. Would it be accepted, embraced, and seen as funny to them? When humor hurts, it creates defensiveness and hinders learning.

- Avoid off-color or sexist jokes. Much adult humor is of this type, but it can stifle the creative spirit. Strive for humor that creates a dynamic, positive flow.

- Use humor that fits your style. When you try to be funny in ways that do not suit your natural personality or delivery style, it can fall flat. If you have a dry sense of humor, develop and use it. If you tend to forget punch lines, avoid telling jokes.

- Let the group discover what's funny. Most groups you teach have a general sense of appropriate humor, so take your cues from them.

- Use humor that directly relates to the topic or enhances learning.

- Use humor indirectly. Use it to put people at ease, to help get people acquainted, and to build relationships.

Use the kind of humor that fits you, but the important thing is to permit and promote humor in your training programs because it creates a wonderfully charged atmosphere for learning. Table 4-1 outlines the many ways that humor asserts a positive influence on the learning experience.

The following tactics will help you add humor to your classes and presentations.

## Table 4-1. How Humor Aids Learning

- Humor relaxes people.
- Humor puts people in a good mood to learn.
- Humor opens the mind.
- Humor makes people more alert.
- Humor builds rapport and breaks down relationship barriers.
- Humor invites participation by increasing the positive energy level.
- Humor dissipates fears and disarms us.
- Humor is known to aid in healing and wholeness.
- Humor makes difficult tasks easier—"A spoonful of sugar helps the medicine go down."
- Humor gets the point across.

## Tactic 12.1: Surprises

**Purpose:** Uses surprises to promote humor.

**Description:** A favorite warm-up is to have people tell their life stories to each other in one minute. Participants often laugh in surprise when they hear the assignment. Surprise gifts, unusual decorations, quirky activities, or unique noises that signal a change in activity add a personal touch of humor.

## Tactic 12.2: The Class Clown

**Purpose:** Allows learners with a good sense of humor to thrive.

**Description:** Participants who have a keen sense of humor often add greatly to the class or workshop. They are usually the ones with high "social intelligence" and know when comic relief is needed. Off-the-cuff humor, side comments, and puns break up potential monotony and keep things light. You can communicate acceptance of such antics through your own smiles and laughter.

## Tactic 12.3: Anecdotes and Stories

**Purpose:** Promotes learning through humorous stories.

**Description:** People remember stories. Funny stories are told repeatedly—what a way to make learning last. You can read stories, tell them, or elicit them from the participants. "Does anyone have a story to tell about...?" (See Tactic 11.6 for some topic ideas.)

### Tactic 12.4: Skits, Stunts, and Dramas

**Purpose:** Uses skits, stunts, and dramas to promote humor in learning.

**Description:** Once adults feel comfortable with each other, they will create wonderfully funny skits and dramas together. Both actors and audiences enjoy this. A teaching topic can come alive when it is dramatized. Stunts can be used to loosen people up and get them laughing as they test their dexterity. Such antics elicit spontaneous laughter, quickly loosening things up.

### Tactic 12.5: Songs and Chants

**Purpose:** Uses songs and chants to promote humor in learning.

**Description:** Funny songs or chants with motions get people to move, breathe, and laugh. Individuals or small groups can compose songs or invent chants right on the spot. You can also lead songs or chants to get things started. One of the authors used this chant to introduce lessons for university students learning English in China:

> *We will speak to be understood.*
> *We will listen to understand.*
> *We are learning English now!*

It energized the participants as well as reinforced the goal of each class.

### Tactic 12.6: Games and Activities

**Purpose:** Uses games and activities to promote humor.

**Description:** Games and activities are a sure way to get learners to lighten up. Table games, interactive games, active team games, or contests help people have fun, laugh, and build relationships. Use games that support the training content and be ready with alternatives. Some instructors like to place puzzles or games on the tables for learners to play. Use caution—these gimmicks can distract, too.

##  Spontaneous Strategy 13: Use Imagination and the Arts

Creative arts awaken our emotions, give us pause, startle us, and bring us gently or starkly to new concepts and ideas. They allow us to use our imaginations as we learn. Art contains elements of unpredictability and surprise, two characteristics that make it an excellent teaching tool suitable for the spontaneous instructor style.

The following tactics will bring the arts into your teaching and allow learners to use their imaginations to grasp the content.

### Tactic 13.1: Music and Singing

**Purpose:** Supports spontaneity with music.

**Description:** Have music playing when participants arrive at your workshop or class. You may want to select music to set a certain mood (light and happy, calming, rousing, and so forth) or to fit the theme of your instruction. Keep a variety of music from which to choose. Participants can learn by singing songs, too. You may have a theme song or make up words to a familiar tune that emphasizes your point. You can also use songs that small groups make up to summarize what participants have learned. Ask each group to sing their special composition as a way to wrap up the session.

### Tactic 13.2: Dance and Creative Movement

**Purpose:** Supports spontaneity with dance and creative movement.

**Description:** Dance or movement can be used as warm-up exercises to energize your participants. Simple circle dances draw a group together. For example, you can use movement that "weaves" a line of people together to teach the importance of community and team work. Put on some music or make up a chant and have the group form a line holding hands. As the music is played or sung, the leader pulls the line along into a weaving that gets tighter and tighter. If the movement is simple and fits the theme, most participants will join in and enjoy it. Allow those who don't wish to participate to stand out and clap or otherwise encourage others.

### Tactic 13.3: Drama

**Purpose:** Supports spontaneity with drama.

**Description:** Use role plays and skits to demonstrate learning. Some trainers hire professional actors to act out roles of clients or customers, which allows participants to witness skills being applied in a realistic setting. Drama can also be used as a catalyst for discussion. You can use participant-actors to portray scenes that spark discussion and enhance learning.

To help learners feel more comfortable, let them practice their roles sufficiently or use small groups for role play. You can also provide a scripted dialogue and allow the actors to interpret the roles the way they want.

### Tactic 13.4: Painting and Drawing

**Purpose:** Supports spontaneity with painting and drawing.

**Description:** Painting and drawing can be done individually or in small groups. Murals can be drawn or painted to express part of the learning theme. You can use paintings and drawings to illustrate points or stimulate discussion. Individual participants can be asked to create drawings to portray ideas or feelings about the training content. You may want to provide them with small drawing pads so they can illustrate their ideas by doodling or sketching during the class. At the end of the workshop, ask participants to share their sketches as a way to summarize the workshop content.

## Tactic 13.5: Decorative Posters and Signs

**Purpose:** Supports spontaneity with visual aids.

**Description:** You can create signs, posters, and flipcharts that contain key points from the training content (or have them made). Display them around the classroom or have learners take them home. These take-home signs can be used as reminders of things learned. Even one-word reminders on cards can be helpful.

## Tactic 13.6: Collage

**Purpose:** Supports spontaneity through collage.

**Description:** Making collages are popular because they are so easy and fun to do. With a little encouragement, participants will make use of all kinds of materials to express ideas and concepts that they are learning. You need some kind of backing (cardboard, construction paper), glue or tape, magazines, and various objects such as ribbon, stickers, colored paper, and so forth. Be clear about the theme so participants can select appropriate pictures and items to add to the collage. After the creative work, it's time for show-and-tell or show-and-guess!

## Tactic 13.7: Poetry

**Purpose:** Supports spontaneity with poetry.

**Description:** Poetry readings are becoming more popular. You can use poetry as a catalyst for getting learners to think about and react to the lessons you teach. Poetry stirs feelings. You can read poems on your topic to participants as an opener or to make a particular point. Individuals can write poems in response to the lesson or small groups can compose poems to read to the whole class.

An easy form of poetry is called a *lune*. A lune is a simple three-line poem written in this form:

*First line: three words*
*Second line: five words*
*Third line: three words*

There are no syllables to count like in haiku, no rhyming is necessary, but the last line of the lune is what packs the punch. Here is a sample lune for customer service:

> *I listen carefully*
> *Eye on sales and service*
> *Sell myself too*

A good way to remember facts is to rhyme them. Make it a class assignment for each person or small group to write a rhyming poem on some aspect of the class content. To remind adult learners to know their purpose before meeting with a co-worker, they were taught this potent little rhyme:

> *Before you speak,*
> *Know just what you desire:*
> *Is it to inform, inquire,*
> *Influence, or inspire?*

##  Spontaneous Strategy 14: Build in Risk Taking

In order to promote risk taking, you must show that you are willing to take risks yourself. You must be willing to change and grow. Sharing your own struggles and past mistakes with learners encourages them to do the same. You also need to demonstrate an acceptance of learning by trial and error, so that learners feel comfortable making mistakes as they attempt to apply the knowledge and skills being taught.

The following tactics will help participants take risks.

### Tactic 14.1: Meet New People

**Purpose:** Promotes risk taking through get-acquainted exercises.

**Description:** Workshops and classes put us in a position to meet new people. Too often, instructors do not allow participants to meet and interact with each other. Make it a normal part of your instructional routine to get people talking to one another. Rather than the typical exercise of asking participants to say their names and where they are from, ask them to share some important things about themselves with at least one other participant. This not only generates energy and builds relationships; it also moves participants a little out of their comfort zones.

### Tactic 14.2: Self-Disclosure

**Purpose:** Promotes risk taking through self-disclosure.

**Description:** Make it your practice to get people to disclose some things about themselves with others early in the workshop. Because adults are often uncomfortable or afraid to talk about their own lives, try to make it fun and easy to do. One simple and practically foolproof way of doing this is to divide the class into pairs or small groups. Ask that each person answer the question, "What's on your plate, personally or professionally?" (Make sure participants know that this is an optional exercise.) With that one little question, adult learners will immediately begin to talk freely. It provides an opportunity to tell as little or as much as they want, but make sure to put a time limit on it and continue the session. You can also instruct listeners to just listen, not ask questions or give advice.

## Tactic 14.3: Try New Skills

**Purpose:** Promotes taking the risk to try new skills.

**Description:** Trying out new skills involves the risk of failure. When you ask learners to teach each other, they may be nervous about demonstrating their skills in front of peers. You can reduce their anxiety by forming small teams in which participants can try out their new skills and feel supported by their team. Remind teams to encourage each other to take risks and underscore the idea that taking risks leads to personal growth. You need only provide the opportunity; let adult participants decide to take the risk.

## Tactic 14.4: Sharing Ideas

**Purpose:** Promotes risk taking through sharing ideas.

**Description:** Everyone gains when people share ideas. The risk involved with exposing your ideas lies in the fear that your idea may be criticized. Tell participants that once an idea is verbalized, it belongs to the group. That way any idea can be examined, modified, accepted, or rejected as needed without reflecting on the originator.

Adults like to share good ideas. Open by asking participants to write down what advice they would like to give on a particular lesson topic. Afterward, arrange for people to share with the whole class or their small groups. You could also solicit topics of interest from the audience and write these on a flipchart. Ask if there is anyone who could give advice on each topic. Divide the audience into interest groups and let the advice givers share with their group members.

## Tactic 14.5: Performing Before Others

**Purpose:** Promotes risk taking by performing before others.

**Description:** One great thing about in-class learning that is superior to online learning or self-study courses is that you have to perform before a group to some degree, by reading a paper, discussing your ideas, making a group report, or demonstrating a skill. For example, after a group discussion, participants may be asked to report the results. Suggest that each group member take turns making the report or use a team approach where each member makes a portion of a report. Sharing information with an audience of colleagues promotes presentation skills, personal growth, and greater learning.

## Tactic 14.6: Give-and-Take Debates

**Purpose:** Promote risk taking through debate.

**Description:** Debates promote risk taking and learning. Effective instructors skillfully promote this kind of dialogue. We take a risk when we challenge another's ideas because we then have to put forth our own ideas. One easy way to get this kind of discussion going is to prepare some controversial statements that are sure to spark a debate. Read each statement and have participants move to one side of the room or the other based on their response. Then hold a general discussion or break into smaller groups for a dialogue between sides.

## Tactic 14.7: Instructor as Model

**Purpose:** Promotes risk taking through instructor modeling.

**Description:** Encourage taking risks whenever practical and possible by modeling this behavior. There are two ways you can do that. First, share something about yourself and be willing to expose your shortcomings. Adults are more willing to risk change when the instructor is open and honest. We are not talking here about baring your soul on personal issues, but to be honest about your need for continual improvement in the area being studied. Second, show an attitude of acceptance toward participants who make mistakes to impress upon the students that the classroom is a safe place to take risks. For example, if a student uses improper terminology, do not embarrass them by openly correcting them. Speak to the student privately and then teach proper terminology when it can be shared more impersonally.

## Spontaneous Strategy 15: Take Time to Reflect

Arrange a time for silence, quiet reflection, or journaling to integrate new ideas. Restrict distractions and let the learners become inwardly spontaneous. Time spent in silence alone or with others can be some of the most productive moments in learning. At these times, thoughts are evoked and our cauldron of ideas stirred. Resist the temptation to fill every moment with words or activity. Silence, as the old saying goes, is golden!

If you can, find a room with natural lighting and plenty of windows. The room should not have piped-in elevator music or other white noise such as loud heating or cooling units, or distracting décor. Ask participants to silence their mobile devices. Turn off computers. This kind of environment is more conducive to quiet reflection on the training content.

The following tactics will help your learners reflect.

## Tactic 15.1: Take Breaks

**Purpose:** Uses breaks to allow learners time to reflect.

**Description:** Breaks are most welcome to participants. Breaks allow them to think, discuss, and react to what went on in the session. Scheduled breaks are good but you can also take spontaneous short breaks or stretch breaks. If you have people moving and working in small groups, tell them to take a personal break whenever they feel like it. Think of breaks as integral to your teaching. If you want to know if the group is ready for a break ask, "Are there any questions?" If not, it could be time for a break.

## Tactic 15.2: Journaling

**Purpose:** Promotes reflection through writing.

**Description:** When you use journal writing in workshops, make a clear distinction between "note-taking" and "journaling." Note-taking is recording the workshop content, whereas journaling records the thoughts and feelings of participants in response to the learning experience. You can offer learners a special book or pad to use just for journaling, instead of to their own note-taking papers or devices. If you have handouts throughout the lesson, make spaces on them for students to write their own thoughts; label the space "Your Ideas."

## Tactic 15.3: Time Between Sessions

**Purpose:** Promotes reflection between sessions.

**Description:** Design activities that require quiet reflection, and ask learners to complete them between sessions.

## Tactic 15.4: Meditation

**Purpose:** Promotes reflection through meditation.

**Description:** Meditation can be taught as a four-step process: relax, release, receive, and respond. Relax: Get comfortable, take deep breaths. Release: Let go of all extraneous thoughts and worries. Receive: Open your mind to all you are learning, seek ways to apply it in your life and work. Respond: Tell others about your insights or write in your journal about them.

## Tactic 15.5: Breathing

**Purpose:** Promotes reflection through deep breathing.

**Description:** Here is a way to use breathing to promote reflection. Good breathing helps one to relax and focus. These are important elements in listening to and organizing one's thoughts, which in turn aids learning. First, simply become aware of your breathing (usually it is shallow chest breathing). Second, sit comfortably, relax, and exhale completely. Here are the steps for deep breathing:

- Breathe in by pushing out your stomach and filling your abdomen with air until full, then fill your chest with air; count slowly to 10 while doing this.

- Hold the breath in for the count of five.

- Slowly exhale to the count of 10.

- Hold the breath out for a count of five.

- Repeat the sequence four or five times. This slow, rhythmic breathing soothes, calms, and reduces anxiety. This could be done in preparation for sessions or after sessions.

## Tactic 15.6: Thought Stimulators

**Purpose:** Promotes reflection by using "thought stimulators."

**Description:** Thought stimulators can be questions, lecturettes, readings, or even a single word that sparks reflection. You can also ask learners to recall a time when they made a unique contribution to their work unit or their field of endeavor. A simple, well-timed question can open a participant's mind to new worlds of thought, feeling, and learning.

Adult learners appreciate it when learning includes fun, surprise, and an element of risk. They also need time to collect their thoughts and use their imaginations. Enjoyable and spontaneous learning, achieved through the strategies and tactics presented here, creates an atmosphere of freedom and creativity. In the next chapter you will learn some ways to help participants feel safe and comfortable in the learning environment.

# 5. The Safe Instructor Style

Adults need to be in a comfortable, trust-filled learning environment to let go of the old and embrace the new. When adults feel accepted and know that their comfort zones are respected, they will drop their guards and relax. When they are certain they won't be judged, they will be more comfortable making necessary growth-producing mistakes. The safe strategies and learning tactics in this chapter will help you design instruction so participants trust you, each other, and your instruction.

Safe strategies include the following:

- Help participants feel at home.
- Let participants know what to expect.
- Help participants get acquainted.
- Keep time commitments.
- Build trust and openness.

##  Safe Strategy 16: Help Participants Feel at Home

The learning space should help participants feel relaxed and welcome. Pay attention to creature comforts such as seating arrangements, refreshments, comfortable temperature and lighting, and restrooms. Welcome participants with visual images that reflect the theme of the class. You may be forced to use facilities with less than desirable conditions, but try to make them comfortable. Create a space that makes it easy for participants to interact. Also give some thought to pleasing all the senses: sight, hearing, smell, touch, and taste.

Pay attention to what the physical space communicates to your adult participants. Does it welcome them or does it feel forbidding? A learning environment should communicate the following seven assurances.

- You are welcome.
- You are important.
- You will be comfortable.
- You will enjoy yourself.
- You will learn.
- You will make friends.
- You will be safe.

The following tactics will help learners feel at home.

## Tactic 16.1: Early Planning

**Purpose:** Promotes preparation to prevent problems.

**Description:** Sometimes you cannot predict what you might find when you arrive to teach at an unfamiliar site. Arrive early to scrutinize the site and make adjustments. Work with hosting services or make what changes you can to assure maximum comfort. Keep in mind the kind of atmosphere you want. Draw attention to the "front" of the room with displays, flipcharts, or with the use of audiovisual equipment. Check the traffic flow to avoid placing obstacles in the path of people entering or exiting the room. Pay attention to lighting, glare from the sun, and electrical outlet placement. The more prepared you are, the more effective you will be. When you are in a pinch for time, involve early arriving participants to help you set up. Be alert to special needs such as language interpreters and wheelchair accessibility. Avoid facilities for workshops where wheelchair accessibility is through a back door or through utility areas.

## Tactic 16.2: Personal Greeting

**Purpose:** Provides friendly human contact as participants enter.

**Description:** When leading a workshop, set things up early so you are free to greet participants as they arrive. You want adult participants to feel welcomed. Volunteers or early arriving participants can also fulfill this role. Participants may have questions or concerns that can be resolved before the class begins. As you greet participants, use that time to find out why they came so you can make the experience as meaningful to them as possible. Even if you teach an ongoing class, it is still a good idea to arrive early for each session, greet participants, and get to know them better.

## Tactic 16.3: Welcoming Environment

**Purpose:** Helps instructors make the learning environment inviting.

**Description:** Think about what welcomes you into a learning space. Attractive and informative posters, the smell of freshly brewed coffee and tea, and tasty snacks are a few things that give a friendly welcome. The room should be prepared with tables and chairs arranged for instruction. Adult participants also enjoy soothing or upbeat music as they arrive in a workshop or class. Music is inviting and can build a sense of community. Be sensitive to your group and try to choose music that most everyone enjoys—avoid extremes.

There will always be certain elements of the physical setting that are beyond your control. Be resourceful in making what improvements you can—the important thing is to show participants that you have taken the time to provide them with a welcoming learning environment.

## Tactic 16.4: Displays

**Purpose:** Provides a center of interest.

**Description:** Display books and materials that are related to your topic invite participants to explore further. Create a center of interest with photographs, automatic slide shows, or other vibrant objects that reinforce the training content. A display also provides a way to immediately engage participants in learning, especially those who are not so gregarious. If you have table groups, you can use the tabletops for displaying materials of interest. Make it fun by allowing groups to create their own displays.

## Tactic 16.5: Seating

**Purpose:** Use the seating arrangement to welcome participants.

**Description:** One good way to welcome participants is to have them enter a room already set up for small groups. Create table groupings for three to five participants. If the group is very large, rows of chairs are more practical to start with, but then quickly have participants move into groups. Moveable chairs are best for this but you may have to disconnect interlocking chairs—the time and energy is worth it. Classrooms full of student desks are relatively moveable and can be rearranged into small groups.

## Tactic 16.6: Add Your Personal Touch

**Purpose:** Makes participants welcome with personal touches from the instructor.

**Description:** You may want to adorn your classroom in ways unique to you. Some instructors put toys or candies on each table for participants. Put culturally diverse posters on the walls or use patterned tablecloths to provide a festive touch. You can also transform poor surroundings with flowers. Unique touches might reflect your particular instruction style or the content of the learning experience.

##  Safe Strategy 17: Let Participants Know What to Expect

Provide participants with clear information about the training event: the objectives, requirements, agenda, dates and schedule, place, instructors, format, and cost. Encourage participants to discuss and negotiate various aspects of the program to arrive at a program that meets their learning needs.

Developing a partnership between instructor and participant is an important aspect of working with adults. A partnership can take place when each side knows what to expect from the other. That is not to say surprises or spontaneous twists and turns cannot take place, but avoid being needlessly sidetracked in ways that will waste time and energy. This will also lessen participants' trust in you. The following are guidelines and practices to develop this partnership in learning.

- Listen to your participants. Gather as much information as possible to understand what their expectations are. You may have little time to do this if the workshop is short, but you can spend a few minutes getting feedback from participants about what they wish to learn. Refer back to chapter 2, "The Systematic Instructor Style," and the strategy *Collaborate With Learners as You Plan*. If you haven't already done so, contact some participants ahead of time, and form them into a focus group to gather information. If you are teaching a class with multiple sessions, find out what participants expect in the first session and periodically check to find out if the content is meeting their expectations. Anonymity may be needed to get honest responses. You can use a "name optional" survey, or request that participants meet together without you and write a summary of their reactions.

- Be honest and realistic about what you are offering to participants. Too often, particularly in short courses and workshops, too little information is provided about what is going to happen. Titles and descriptions of these classes often do not fully explain the agenda. To reduce anxiety and confusion—an important part of the safe instructor style—provide a detailed description of content as well as a complete agenda. Explain the syllabus clearly and, if change is needed, be honest about it.

- Come to an agreement. Bring the agenda discussion to closure by coming to an agreement. Usually just getting a nod of affirmation by the group is enough. "So we have agreed to have a break every hour on the hour, right?" In situations that are more complex, a written agreement may be necessary, such as on a flipchart sheet or on an overhead. It is essential to publicly acknowledge what decisions have been reached and seal the understanding with some symbol of agreement. And, of course, you must keep the agreement.

The following tactics will help learners know what to expect from you.

## Tactic 17.1: Share Basic Instructional Information

**Purpose:** Provides participants with basic instructional information.

**Description:** Here is a list of important information you might share with participants before getting started:

- course objectives
- basic course content
- course requirements
- agenda or schedule
- methods of instruction
- your expectation of participation
- fees
- registration information
- background and qualifications of the instructor
- requirements to complete the class.

## Tactic 17.2: Housekeeping

**Purpose:** Provides information about the physical space and administrative regulations and proceedings.

**Description:** Providing information about the things on this list will enhance participant comfort and well-being:

- restroom and telephone location
- snacks
- breaks
- meals

- site rules—off-limit areas, equipment usage, and so on
- special-needs access
- displays/resources
- smoking policy
- local opportunities—walks, trails, shopping, and so forth
- special events
- breakout rooms
- name tags.

## Tactic 17.3: Special Needs

**Purpose:** Informs participants of arrangements for meeting special needs.

**Description:** Will there be a need for a language or sign language interpreter? Will there be physical barriers that must be explained? What about literacy demands? Will participants be asked to read aloud? Gain as much information about what is required by participants with special needs and try to find resources to meet these needs. If possible, inform people with special needs in advance if you cannot provide what they need.

## Tactic 17.4: Diversity

**Purpose:** Demonstrates appreciation of diversity among participants.

**Description:** Your communication prior to the training event should include assurance that you are sensitive to and appreciate the diversity of your participants. Assure participants that your class does not discriminate based on ethnicity, culture, gender, or sexual preference. Your instruction and instructional materials should present a nonbiased viewpoint with respect to cultural and religious beliefs.

## Tactic 17.5: What to Bring

**Purpose:** Informs participants of what they need to bring with them to the training event.

**Description:** The list of items to bring may not be as long as the one you got when you went to summer camp, but participants should be told what they are expected to bring. These might include any prework you may have assigned, or sample business records for study. Items can also include those necessary for participants' physical comfort: a sweater, water, coffee, snacks, or lunches. It's a good idea to bring some extra items just in case someone forgets—no one likes to be the oddball. Help everyone come prepared.

## Tactic 17.6: Changes

**Purpose:** Informs participants of changes as soon as possible.

**Description:** It is disconcerting and disruptive when changes are made and participants are not informed. You do not want participants arriving at an empty room with no sign to guide them to the new location. If you plan changes in your curriculum or agenda, inform participants about it ahead of time. When participants know what to expect, tension about changes often dissipates. Try to have *planned* surprises only.

## Tactic 17.7: Be Flexible

**Purpose:** Encourages flexibility in meeting expectations.

**Description:** Can you adjust your plan? If not, you may not want to teach adults. Various factors, including time constraints, an inability to meet specific requests, or other limits may force you to change or adapt your instructional plan or physical setting. Be prepared for these kinds of disruptions. When there is a problem, involve the participants in solving it—and make sure everyone understands the new plan.

#  Safe Strategy 18: Help Participants Get Acquainted

Plan get-acquainted exercises so participants can become familiar with each other, the topic, and the instructor. Devise a way to get adults actively involved with each other early on but show sensitivity to participants' comfort zones. The best use of time is to combine topic-related activities with interpersonal connections. You are trying to build a sense of trust between adults and at the same time raise interest in the program.

Get-acquainted exercises are often left off the agenda because they may seem frivolous and extraneous to learning. Quite the contrary! We are social beings and influenced by others, so interaction is central to learning.

You must gauge your activities to your participants, however. You want them to feel comfortable and not anxious, so select your warm-up activities carefully to help build bridges with your audience. If instructors are confident and know why getting-acquainted exercises are so important, they will find little resistance to them by adult participants.

People like to tell stories and talk about themselves. When participants reveal aspects of their lives, acceptance and appreciation shown by the group helps individuals feel less threatened. Avoid the large group "go-around" introductions so commonly used. Such exercises usually just end up increasing participants' anxiety. They do not listen to others because they are too busy preparing for or recovering from their own presentation. In most cases it is not necessary that everyone get to know about everybody else.

Instead we suggest small group get-acquainted exercises that:

- Build rapport and cooperation.
- Help learners discover their common needs and problems.
- Stimulate creativity.

Here are some principles that guide get-acquainted and warm-up exercises:

- About 25 percent of the session time should be devoted to helping people get ready to learn.
- Give participants freedom to "pass" on any activity if they would rather not participate.
- Explain to participants what you are doing and why you are doing it. Seek general agreement before proceeding.
- Choose get-acquainted exercises that clearly support the learning objectives. If feasible, join the group in get-acquainted exercises.
- Choose get-acquainted exercises that also introduce the topic.

The following tactics help participants get acquainted.

## Tactic 18.1: Tell Your Life Story in One Minute

**Purpose:** Promotes getting acquainted quickly.

**Description:**

1. Form groups of two to four people.
2. While one person in each group keeps time, participants take turns telling their life stories in one minute.
3. After all have shared, let groups explore any interesting bits of information gleaned from the exchange. You may also assign a theme to the sharing—share your career life story, education life story, or life story as it relates to the lesson.

## Tactic 18.2: I Imagine You...

**Purpose:** Helps participants who are somewhat acquainted to learn more about others in the group.

**Description:**

1. Form groups of two to four people.
2. Ask participants to choose partners. Partners tell each other what they imagine they each were like in sixth grade, junior high, or as an entry-level employee.

3. Ask participants to then reveal a true description of themselves and compare that with their partners' imagined one.

## Tactic 18.3: I Want to Know...

**Purpose:** Lets participants decide what they want to know about others.

**Description:**

1. Group size can vary.

2. Start by having each person write down several questions they want to know about others in the group.

3. Let the group mill around. When you give a signal, have them stop and face the nearest person.

4. Each person then asks the other a question from the list and gets a response. Signal to start the group milling again. Repeat the process as often as you like. Or, instead of questions, ask participants to share something about themselves: their jobs, three wishes they have, what they would do with a million dollars, or what they want to learn today.

## Tactic 18.4: License Plate

**Purpose:** Captures the essence of a person quickly.

**Description:**

1. Form groups of four to six people.

2. Have participants imagine they are creating a license plate (only seven letters and numbers may be used) that expresses their personality or a prominent aspect of their lives.

3. Ask participants to share their license plates with the group for discussion.

## Tactic 18.5: Role Call

**Purpose:** Helps the instructor and other participants learn why people have come to the class.

**Description:**

1. Use in groups of up to 30. (Add volunteer facilitators if the group is larger than 30.)

2. Use a flipchart, overhead, or whiteboard—more than one if needed.

3. As people enter the room for the first time, ask them what they do that brings them to this gathering.

4.  Make a list of each role on the flipchart and add slash marks for repeat answers.

5.  Encourage participants to talk with each other as the group gradually grows.

6.  Review the results of the role call when all have gathered.

Or, instead of roles, find out other interesting facts about participants; or add what they each came to learn to their roles.

## Tactic 18.6: I Wish...

**Purpose:** Solicits expectations from the group.

**Description:**

1.  Form groups of two to five people.

2.  Have groups answer these two questions: "What do you wish would happen in this session?" and "What do you wish would not happen?" Ask them to record their answers.

3.  Groups report their answers and the instructor helps them clarify each point if necessary.

4.  Contract with the group to meet agreed-on expectations.

5.  At the end of the session review the lists to ensure expectations were met.

More get-acquainted exercises are described in Table 5-1.

##  Safe Strategy 19: Keep Time Commitments

There is nothing more irritating and distracting than to be in a meeting or training session and realize that the leader has lost track of the time. Participants fidget, look at watches, and generally suffer in silence. Instructors should try to stick to the original schedule. Balance the schedule between the need to cover all the material listed on the agenda, and the needs of participants to spend more time on various parts of the lesson. Help participants understand what is at stake if they arrive late to the session or take extended breaks.

You can show respect to your participants by following these guidelines.

## Table 5-1. Some More Ways to Get Acquainted

**You Are Unique:**
Have each participant share something no one knows about him.

**No Social Props:**
Have participants introduce themselves to each other without mentioning any roles they fill (they can't reveal their job titles, parent roles, or positions in volunteer organizations).

**Who's Here Cheer:**
Have a set of variables ready (type of job, job roles, goals for the training event, places of origin, and so forth). As you name them, participants can stand and cheer if they fall into any of the categories.

## Tactic 19.1: Budget Your Time

**Purpose:** Promotes good planning.

**Description:** Rehearse every part of a workshop or class to get a general idea of how much time the various components or activities will take. If it looks like you are squeezed for time (the most common problem), modify or eliminate sections. Then write out a schedule listing your targeted times. If you tend to go off on tangents or lose track of time, appoint a timekeeper to keep things flowing.

## Tactic 19.2: Begin and End on Time

**Purpose:** Helps keep beginning and ending time commitments.

**Description:** Instructors need to be early! Prepare ahead of time so you can begin on time. Reward the people who come on time by answering some of their immediate questions while you wait for latecomers. Adults are most perturbed when classes end late. In fact, they want to get out early, so design your session with that as a goal. If adults are checking their watches anxiously, your instruction may be for naught. One instructor we know always times his training so that he can announce, "We'll be finished early," thus winning the hearts of his learners.

### Tactic 19.3: Transition Time

**Purpose:** Allows for participant "nesting" needs.

**Description:** When participants have to travel far or rush between sessions, it helps to give them a little time for transition. This is a basic need that can be thought of as human "nesting" time—we all need to settle down and get personally oriented from one situation to another. Casual conversation, networking with others, sipping drinks, or eating snacks fulfills this need.

### Tactic 19.4: Keep Control Kindly

**Purpose:** Keeps the training on track by using gentle reminders.

**Description:** Let guest speakers know how much time they have to speak. Do not leave time allotments vague. Stand where participants will not see you so you can, if necessary, signal the speaker with the "time" sign. To verbose participants, simply and kindly say, "Thanks, but we need to move on," and do so with resolve. If you are kind and firm in keeping control, everyone will be happy. Some instructors like to use the "parking lot," which is a place to list unplanned topics that come up. The idea is to come back to these if time permits.

### Tactic 19.5: Publish the Agenda

**Purpose:** Informs participants in writing of timelines.

**Description:** Always remember to publish an agenda for participants. No matter how informal the gathering or how short the session, always have an agenda. Participants need to know what will happen and when. The agenda need not be very detailed, but there should be a list of general topics and a timeline. You can write the agenda on the whiteboard, or in a handout, and always email it to participants ahead of time. Again, if it needs to change, inform participants as soon as possible.

### Tactic 19.6: Breaks

**Purpose:** Manages breaks for participant and instructor needs.

**Description:** Breaks are sacred. If you have published them as part of your plan, adhere to them religiously unless you have renegotiated break time with participants at the start of the workshop. Breaks can be scheduled or left up to the group to decide when there is a need. It is important to remind participants when the break is over. Breaks and lunch may be incorporated into the training program. Send learners off to lunch with an assignment that involves interacting with other participants.

### Tactic 19.7: Getting Back on Track

**Purpose:** Allows flexibility while keeping the session on track.

**Description:** Sometimes it is advantageous to stray temporarily from the agenda in the interest of following a thread that is vital to the learning experience (we discuss the importance of this in the chapter on the spontaneous instructor style). But when you are ready to get back on track, here are some suggestions for doing so:

- Ask participants to be alert when things get off track and say so.

- State clearly the discrepancy between the plan and the current situation and be clear about the instructional consequences of straying from it.

- Pay attention to the participants who seem uncomfortable with the diversion and ask for their opinions.

##  Safe Strategy 20: Build Trust and Openness

Participants build better relationships with each other through mutual problem solving and discussion. Form small groups, when practical, to encourage the free flow of ideas. Trust takes time to build, so it is best to keep small groups together over an extended period of time.

In a "Be a Better Listener" class, participants work in triads. One of them listens, one observes, and one speaks—they take turns in rotation. After an explanation about maintaining confidentiality, the participants are encouraged to talk about real problems in their lives. People have walked away amazed that they were able to be so candid with strangers and often find that they have received valuable help in the exchange.

Learning has been a breeding ground for many negative feelings. Fear and anxiety and even anger can be triggered by a learning task. Will I measure up? Will I be judged unfairly by the teacher? Will I be put on the spot? Will I be embarrassed or humiliated? Performance anxiety is almost universal in our competitive society. We build it into everything.

You might think adults would feel self-assured and confident in learning new things because they have been learning all their lives. But for most of us, our learning experiences have been in schools and colleges—formal educational settings. In that environment, learning was demanded, not encouraged. Grades reflected a certain level of performance. Expectations from teachers, peers, and parents, combined with the demands we put on ourselves, often created pressure and conflict. Instructors can do much to minimize performance anxiety by using strategies that reassure adult learners.

The following strategies help participants build openness and trust.

## Tactic 20.1: Emphasize the Importance of Confidentiality

**Purpose:** Helps participants keep confidences when needed.

**Description:** Some classroom discussions are better when you stress the need to treat as confidential anything heard within the course of the learning experience. This is one of the items listed in Table 5-2. Confidentiality encourages honest sharing and, when it is stressed, adults are most willing to comply.

### Table 5-2. Rules for Safe Learning

- You are free "to pass."
- Judge ideas, not people.
- Be a good active listener.
- Keep personal confidences.
- Encourage each other to take risks.
- Accept mistakes as part of the learning process.

## Tactic 20.2: The Instructor's Attitude Counts

**Purpose:** Communicates enthusiasm for learning.

**Description:** Do you enjoy learning? Are you looking forward to this experience? Your excitement about the learning experience will help your participants catch the mood. Know and believe in what you are about to teach. Do you have a clear picture of your objectives? Have you prepared learning activities that will accomplish the objectives? Do you believe the learning experience will benefit the participants? Your belief in your objectives and methods will translate into a confident demeanor that will put your participants at ease—even if, inwardly, you are a little nervous. By the way, do not be afraid to say that you are nervous. It will serve as proof of your honesty to participants. But check out the breathing technique discussed in Tactic 15.5 for a way to reduce your anxiety.

## Tactic 20.3: Be a Good Listener

**Purpose:** Promotes listening to participants.

**Description:** When we are listened to, we trust. The instructor needs to model good listening skills and teach participants to listen carefully to each other. If a participant has a soft voice, move closer for better hearing. You may tell participants that they are free to make side comments to one another while you talk, but to listen very closely to their fellow participants when they talk. If too much side talking gets to be an issue, acknowledge it and facilitate a solution.

## Tactic 20.4: Small Group Sharing

**Purpose:** Uses small group sharing to build trust.

**Description:** Small groups simulate a family unit, which may be why they are such a powerful force in promoting learning and personal growth. The use of triads or groups of three participants is an excellent instruction tool. (See Table 5-3.) Remember that keeping groups together over time promotes greater trust.

### Table 5-3. 10 Reasons for Using Groups of Three in Teaching Adults

1.  Intimacy: The group is small enough to encourage intimacy and personal disclosure.
2.  Discussion: The group is large enough to allow for lively discussion and for harboring multiple points of view.
3.  Fairness: Each member can contribute with less chance for domination by any member.
4.  Bonding: The group size promotes cohesion among members. It simulates a family unit.
5.  Combinations: The triad can easily be combined with other triads to form larger groups for other purposes.
6.  Learning Roles: It accommodates basic learner roles such as observer/recorder, listener/receiver, and speaker/actor.
7.  Safety: The group size minimizes embarrassment in exercises like role playing and practicing new skills.
8.  Flexibility: It is a good unit to form in large or small training workshops. In large groups, the triad promotes intimacy. In smaller groups, it allows for inter-group activities.
9.  Cooperation: The odd number helps avoid stalemates in decision making.
10. Mobility/Scheduling: A group of three can easily move around for training exercises and members can coordinate personal schedules for out-of-session assignments.

## Tactic 20.5: Working and Playing Together

**Purpose:** Builds trust through mutual activities.

**Description:** A powerful bond develops when people accomplish or create things together. Plan to involve groups in problem solving, working, and playing together. Participants can form teams to compete in a learning game or cooperate on a group project. When groups support their members in these activities, they will reach their goals successfully and experience a satisfying, energizing, and motivating way to learn and grow.

## Tactic 20.6: Respect What They Know

**Purpose:** Builds trust by respecting what participants already know.

**Description:** A maxim to follow—do not insult your participants' intelligence. At the beginning of a class or workshop, make an effort to assess participants' existing skills and knowledge—use an exercise such as in Tactic 18.1. Design your class so that more advanced participants gain recognition and perhaps take on the role of mentor to others. Also, you might consider referring to your lecturettes as information for some and a review for others. Most adults appreciate a review of previously learned knowledge.

## Tactic 20.7: Model Openness and Trust

**Purpose:** Reminds instructors to set the tone for openness.

**Description:** Probably the most potent way to encourage trust and openness in participants is to model it. Acknowledge your past mistakes and your own struggles to achieve your current level of knowledge and skill. Share personal information and opinions to some degree so that participants can identify with you.

At the same time, trust that your participants want to learn and grow. Trust them to be diligent and responsible, and realize that they are works in progress just as you are. Teaching is a give-and-take relationship that aims for mutual growth in understanding, knowledge, and skill. Here is another maxim, attributed to Alison King: Go "from sage on the stage, to guide on the side."

# 6. Planning for Balanced Instruction

In a previous chapter, we made a distinction between the terms *style*, *strategy*, and *activity*. This chapter contains a sample workshop that *blends the strategies* of each instructor style to create a balanced teaching plan. Chapter 7 will show you how to create your own teaching plan using a blend of strategies and activities from each of the four instructor styles.

## Balance Is Best

To properly employ the four instructor styles and ensure the best learning experience for your participants, you must make sure the styles operate in balance. Participants should benefit equally from each style. They will understand the logic of your instruction (systematic), they will be challenged to learn (stimulating), they will experience surprise and humor (spontaneous), and they will feel comfort and trust while learning (safe).

Balance is difficult to achieve if an instructor is not flexible. The two main errors made by instructors are that we teach the way we learn or we teach the way we were taught. We settle for the style of delivery we find most comfortable. For example, one instructor may prefer a logical plan at the expense of more spontaneity. Some instructors may not take enough time to help people feel safe and comfortable because they want to jump right into presenting their ideas. Another instructor may spend too much time and energy on fun and games, and largely ignore a more systematic approach to planning.

As you study the strategies, identify the ones you tend to avoid and those you fall back on, or for which you feel a natural preference. Learning to appreciate and use all 20 strategies will help you achieve creative balance of the instructor styles. Improvement comes with thorough and accurate assessment, critical reflection, and willingness to try new ways. When you examine and diversify the ways you teach, you will better serve your adult participants. Those strategies will most likely be the ones you should use and improve.

# A Planning Sequence

Balancing the four instructor styles can be achieved through a sequence of steps. This chapter presents the steps in detail and uses a sample workshop to help you visualize how the strategies can be combined in planning to create a balanced teaching style. You can use Worksheet 6-1 to record your ideas as you follow these steps.

The recommended planning sequence is as follows:

1.  **Plan Using the Systematic Instructor Style and Strategies.** This step helps you establish the basic objectives and outline for your instructional program.

2.  **Plan Using the Stimulating Instructor Style and Strategies.** This step helps you design a program that meets your instructional objectives.

3.  **Plan Using the Spontaneous Instructor Style and Strategies.** This step helps you devise ways to make the instruction enjoyable and unique.

4.  **Plan Using the Safe Instructor Style and Strategies.** This step helps you comfortably draw participants into the experience you have designed.

# A Sample Workshop: "Lead With Style"

The sample workshop was designed for those in leadership positions in the childcare field. This includes childcare center directors and supervisors—those directly responsible for personnel. The planning for the "Lead With Style" workshop follows the four-step process outlined above.

This sample workshop was designed as a session at a conference for childcare professionals. There are two main aims of this workshop: 1) identifying and balancing one's leadership style, and 2) identifying and correcting imbalance in one's organization. The concepts taught in this workshop mirror those discussed in this book.

## Step One: Plan Using the Systematic Instructor Style and Strategies

In this step you will decide how you will involve participants in the planning. How will you assess the needs of participants? What are their learning objectives? What are the main content points and methods you will use? How will you evaluate the effectiveness of your instruction?

The strategies that will help you incorporate the Systematic Instructor Style include:

*   Collaborate with learners as you plan.

*   Assess participant learning needs and styles.

*   Set clear, meaningful objectives.

- Plan to reach your objectives.

- Evaluate your plan.

## Worksheet 6-1. Instructor Planning Notes

*Use this form to incorporate each instructor style into your sessions. It is best to follow the planning sequence as outlined below.*

GENERAL TOPIC:_____

SUMMARY OF THE MOST IMPORTANT IDEAS TO COVER:

_____

_____

1. SYSTEMATIC: Well-planned and designed cooperatively. How will I assess learning needs? How will I involve participants in the plan? What are the learning objectives? What is my tentative teaching plan? How will I evaluate?

_____

_____

2. STIMULATING: Active learning, new ideas, solves real problems. What new, provocative, or inspiring ideas will I teach? How can I make learning active? How can I help participants solve real problems in their daily lives?

_____

_____

3. SPONTANEOUS: Humor, fun, surprise, reflection. How will I get participants to interact freely? How will I encourage risk taking? How can I introduce fun, surprise, or humor? Should I plan for personal reflection or journaling? If so, how?

_____

_____

4. SAFE: Comfortable learning space, closeness, and trust. How will I design the learning space for comfort? What types of team-building activities will I use? How will I accommodate participant needs?

_____

_____

**1. Collaborate With Learners as You Plan.** The instructor of the "Lead With Style" workshop met with a group of childcare center directors who confirmed that the concepts to be taught in the workshop were relevant to their group. They also provided important information that resulted in some modifications to the design. Collaboration with the childcare conference leaders, who had requested the workshop, also confirmed that the general content was important and should be added to the conference offerings. The class description was listed in the conference brochure and the instructor was confident that it would draw participants who wanted and needed this kind of instruction.

**2. Assess Participant Learning Needs and Styles.** The instructor had no chance to assess the needs of the participants prior to the workshop. Consequently the instructor used three methods for a quick on-site assessment:

1.  As participants arrived, the instructor greeted them and asked them what their job roles were and what they hoped to gain from the workshop. Their answers were recorded on a flipchart for all to see and were reviewed early in the class.

2.  The instructor listed the objectives and the agenda for the workshop and asked participants to indicate agreement or disagreement with them—no one disagreed.

3.  The instructor had the participants spend a few minutes in small groups discussing and reporting what they wished would and would not happen in the workshop. The instructor then clarified and indicated which of their expectations could be met. Most were met and those that could not be met were explained. This created a general mood of pleasant anticipation.

**3. Set Clear, Meaningful Objectives.** The six objectives for the class were based initially on the feedback from a prior meeting with the center directors and from conversations with the conference staff. The objectives were listed on the cover of the workshop handout packet. The feedback from the needs assessment conducted in the first minutes of the workshop showed that the objectives were appropriate and well-targeted for these participants.

"Lead With Style" Workshop Objectives:

- Learn about different leadership styles.

- Identify your leadership style.

- Analyze four elements that contribute to the health of your organization.

- Plan for organizational development.

- Implement a coaching process in your organization.

- Enjoy learning today.

**4. Plan to Reach Your Objectives.** The instructor designed the program based on the six objectives. The instructor presented the leadership styles in a handout and PowerPoint presentation. Participants then determined their style by using an inventory tool that consisted of a words list, similar to the *Instructor Style Inventory* presented in chapter 8. The instructor designed a presentation on the "Elements of a Healthy Organization," based on the four leadership styles (See Table 6-1). This was followed by an analysis of the participants' organizations and any potential changes needed. Next, the group learned about and discussed human change, which was followed by a presentation and practice in employee coaching. Participants interviewed each other as they planned for the changes they saw were needed.

**5. Evaluate Your Plan.** The conference staff had already designed a workshop evaluation that determined how valuable the participants felt the experience was for them. The instructor devised another brief evaluation asking participants to rate to what extent the objectives were met, revisiting the flipcharts from the needs assessment conducted at the beginning of class.

## Step Two: Plan Using the Stimulating Instructor Style and Strategies

In this step the instructor determines how the content will be structured and presented. What new and useful ideas can be taught? What active learning activities can participants engage in? How will you help participants solve real problems they will face? How will you help them practice new skills?

The strategies that will help you incorporate the stimulating instructor style include:

- Present information in interesting, useful ways.

- Use active learning approaches.

- Encourage creativity.

- Help participants solve real problems.

- Help participants practice new learning.

## Table 6-1. Elements of a Healthy Organization

*The following four elements define a "healthy organization." A healthy organization has a clear vision, a strategy that aligns with that vision, encouragement of risk taking and experimentation, and employee commitment and happiness. When these elements are present, you have a dynamic combination that spells success for the organization.*

| STIMULATING (vision and inspiration) | SPONTANEOUS (freedom and experimentation) |
|---|---|
| The organization has to have a vision and people have to own it, love it, and desire it. It is not just something written on a brochure or website; it is integrated into the daily work that goes on in an organization. People are motivated by it; it keeps them working just as much as a paycheck—it is the raison d'être of the organization. | Not all work is creative, but all work can be engaging and enjoyable when workers are encouraged to try new approaches, and are not afraid to make mistakes while trying. Having some freedom and control over one's job makes it fun. Doing what you know how to do makes it fun. The workplace needs to be a place that celebrates and has joy. Laughter abounds in a spontaneous place. People tell stories and jokes. People are free to create, make errors, and experiment. |
| SYSTEMATIC (goals, roles, and resources) | SAFE (trust and acceptance) |
| An effective organization is organized. There is little or no neglected work, under-funded projects, or mismanaged resources. The work flows. If something happens to disrupt this flow, the organization analyzes the disruption and makes appropriate corrections. Workers don't lose time in confusion or misdirection. They understand how their role contributes to organizational goals. The leader takes the lead and keeps things running smoothly. | The healthy organization is a place where people feel comfortable and have a sense of belonging. Undervalued people, people taken for granted, people who do not feel "safe" soon leave or undermine the organization's mission. In a healthy organization, people work across functions and communicate honestly and openly. Leaders listen more than they talk and teach others to listen to each other. |

**6. Present Information in Interesting, Useful Ways.** The content of the workshop was new to the participants. The material was presented through handouts, lecturettes, PowerPoint presentations, and inventories that the participants filled out. Participants felt that the content would help them immediately become more effective in their jobs.

**7. Use Active Learning Approaches.** The instructor used several methods to make sure participants were actively involved in learning. Participants were immediately involved in reviewing and planning the session's objectives.

- Participants were asked to fill out inventories and analyze and discuss them.
- Participants read and discussed material presented in handouts.
- Participants moved around to join small groups and form partners.
- Participants were asked to interview each other using a guide sheet.
- The participants worked together to solve their management problems and create plans for improvement.
- Participants asked questions which were answered by other participants as well as the instructor.
- Only a few minutes were taken for direct instruction.

**8. Encourage Creativity.** The workshop involved having participants work together to solve problems and plan creative changes in their organizations. The instructor facilitated this process so that each participant became a client as well as a consultant. These roles allowed the participants to generate new ways of thinking, organizing, and acting. The structured process of the workshop allowed participants to explore within certain parameters.

**9. Help Participants Solve Real Problems.** The main focus of the workshop was helping childcare directors become more effective leaders. The participants filled out inventories pertaining to their roles as managers, worked on analyzing their organizations' "health," and then applied this information in devising solutions to their problems back on the job.

**10. Help Participants Practice Their Learning.** The directors paired off and held simulated coaching interviews. They focused on improving their management styles and created personal and organizational development plans. If there had been more time, the instructor might have arranged a simulated staff meeting so the participants could have rehearsed some of the planned changes in their management styles. Participants were paired off to follow up with each other on their progress back on the job.

## Step Three: Plan Using the Spontaneous Instructor Style and Strategies

In this step the instructor reviews the curriculum to find room for some "planned spontaneity." How will you help participants share their stories? How will you make the learning experience enjoyable? How could you weave humor into the instruction? Will you integrate times for reflection or journaling? How will you facilitate risk taking for the sake of learning?

The strategies that will help you incorporate the spontaneous instructor style include:

- Help participants tell their stories.
- Make it funny, make it fun.
- Use imagination and the arts.
- Build in risk taking.
- Take time to reflect.

**11. Help Participants Tell Their Stories.** The participants began telling their stories right away when the instructor asked participants to share "what is on your plate" in a warm-up exercise. The participants wanted to talk with others in similar roles; this was a rare opportunity for them. They discussed the results of their personal leadership styles and organizational inventory exercises. This brought out many tales of positive and negative experiences. Participants talked in pairs about the need for change and plans for improvement in their organizations.

**12. Make It Funny, Make It Fun.** The instructor used an activity (the "I wish..." activity described in chapter 5) that provided an opportunity for participants to say what they like and dislike in workshops. Throughout the workshop the instructor used informal humor and bantered with the leaders. The participants laughed and enjoyed themselves as they shared their mutual foibles in management of childcare centers. Just being in similar roles brings out curiosity and humor in learners.

**13. Use Imagination and the Arts.** The instructor played soft but lively music as the participants entered. Later, soft pleasant music was played as participants imagined being back in their work roles. They imagined the positive changes they might experience as they applied what they learned. Given more time, the instructor could have used poetry, sculpture, or collages to help participants visualize changes in their workplaces. For example, participants could have written a poem or song as a small group to illustrate how their organizations might look after certain changes were implemented.

**14. Build in Risk Taking.** The instructor presented opportunities for participants to take the risk of self-disclosure. If these leaders were able to be honest with themselves and others, they could better diagnose their problems and accurately target needed changes in their leadership style and organizational development. Through the "What's on my plate?" exercise, self-disclosures resulted in problem-solving discussions and activities.

**15. Take Time to Reflect.** Participants were given time to reflect after they filled out their individual and organizational inventories. After participants had finished these analyses, they could think about the implications of the results. An optional activity asked participants to begin a journal to be continued on the job as reminder of the insights gained and the commitments they made toward change.

## Step Four: Plan Using the Safe Instructor Style and Strategies

In this step the instructor makes decisions about the best way to help participants feel comfortable and ready to learn. How will you make participants feel at home in the learning environment? How will you tell or show participants what to expect? How will you help participants get acquainted with each other? How will you ensure time commitments are made and met? How will you help participants become trusting and open in your workshop?

The strategies that will help you incorporate the safe instructor style include:

- Help participants feel at home.
- Let participants know what to expect.
- Help participants get acquainted.
- Keep time commitments.
- Build trust and openness.

**16. Help Participants Feel at Home.** The soft, lively music playing, the seating arrangements, and snacks created a pleasant atmosphere. The projector screen showed a photo of a leader and workers raising their hands in solidarity; this brought smiles. Signs in the hall helped participants easily locate the room and a welcome sign was placed near the entrance. The instructor arranged an attractive display of topical books and materials in the front to draw participants in. The instructor warmly greeted each person, and began to conduct brief, informal interviews and recorded on a flipchart each person's role and reasons for attending the workshop. The instructor wanted to create a sense of community and help each participant realize her role in the mutual learning process.

**17. Let Participants Know What to Expect.** After providing some housekeeping details (location of bathroom, timing of breaks, and so forth) and leading a warm-up exercise, the instructor handed each person a packet of materials. The packet included the workshop objectives and agenda, handouts, and participant inventories. The instructor reviewed all of these materials with the class and allowed time for the participants to ask questions or make suggestions. After conducting the needs assessment, the instructor explained which needs would be met (and which wouldn't, and why) and made adjustments to accommodate some requests. Everyone knew what would happen in the session, how they might gain from it, and what was expected of them.

**18. Help Participants Get Acquainted.** The instructor selected three methods for helping the participants get acquainted:

- As they entered, the instructor briefly interviewed each participant and posted her job title and reason for attending the class. This provided a way for participants to see who was attending and why.

- In small groups, participants shared what was happening currently in their lives and work. This allowed participants to disclose, if they wished, their issues at work or home, relieve some stress, and identify with other participants—a great way to build groups.

- Participants shared their expectations and hopes for the class. This gave them a sense of control over the learning experience as well as kicked off the process of group problem solving. At the end of these three activities, the participants were happily talking, working, and laughing together—a good sign that the activities worked.

**19. Keep Time Commitments.** The instructor published the schedule in the workshop packet and on a flipchart. The schedule was followed closely and the break was taken as planned. The instructor also assured participants the class would end a few minutes early and it did. Once dismissed, participants were free to talk with the instructor and look over the display materials. See the "Lead With Style" Workshop Agenda.

**20. Build Trust and Openness.** This workshop relied heavily on small group work and trust building. The get-acquainted exercises formed teams and then participants worked in the same groups to analyze their inventories and work on management and organizational improvements. In fact, for most of the session, the participants worked in small, intimate groups where they felt safe to reveal their problems and solve them with others in the group. The instructor emphasized that the participants all faced difficult assignments in the field of childcare administration, so no one should feel shy in working together toward effective change. The partner interviews in the coaching training also built trust.

## "Lead With Style" Workshop Agenda

**8:30 a.m.**
- Introduction
- Needs Assessment Exercise
- Greetings by Instructor and Role-Call Exercise
- "What's On Your Plate" Exercise
- Distribution and Discussion of Workshop Packets
- "I Wish..." Exercise

**9:15 a.m.**
- Lead With Style
- Lecturette #1: Leadership Styles
- Small Group Discussions
- Lecturette #2: Four Elements of a Healthy Organization
- Small Group Discussions
- Lecturette #3: AIM in Coaching
- Coaching Interviews

**11:15 a.m.**
- Wrap-Up
- Group Problem Solving
- Evaluation

# Summary

The "Lead With Style" workshop offers a real-life example of a training program that uses multiple strategies to achieve balanced instruction. The suggested sequence of steps can be used as a planning guide that will help you incorporate each of the instructor styles and strategies in your own training programs. Chapter 7 offers more information for blending strategies and activities from each of the four instructor styles.

# 7. Practical Application of the Model

The preceding chapters provide a general understanding of the Teach With Style model. This chapter shows you how to implement the model, using another workshop as an example. It shows how specific learning tactics can be selected to provide an interesting and useful program for participants. Use your imagination as you read to place yourself in the roles of both instructor and learner. Think about how you would react to each tactic as a learner. How would you make it better? How would you tailor it to fit your unique needs? As an instructor, how might you apply it to other subjects you teach? What other learning tactics might you use to enhance the learning experience or to balance your approach? Create a matrix similar to the one in Table 7-2 to see if you are indeed balanced in your approach. This is a great way to see if you are relying too heavily on a particular style!

## Sample Workshop: "Delivering Effective Presentations"

This workshop is designed for those who want to improve their presentation skills. Many of us are faced with the challenge of standing up in front of a group, whether it is a college project, presenting to our co-workers, or in volunteer positions where we are called upon to lead. In this workshop learners observe an example of an effective presentation and discover how to achieve the positive results of that presenter. Mixed in the workshop are opportunities for each student to learn how to organize their content for an engaging presentation, how to avoid the habits of a "bad" presenter, and how to practice the skills that are taught in the short workshop. This example demonstrates how to use specific learning tactics, which are summarized in Tables 7-1 and 7-2.

**Table 7-1. "Delivering Effective Presentations" Half-Day Workshop**

| Topic | Objective | Activity/Content | Materials |
|---|---|---|---|
| Instructor intro and course overview | Participants will gain an understanding of the course goals. | Instructor will discuss his expertise and review the agenda. | Syllabus, agenda poster, PowerPoint slide of instructor credentials |
| 30-second presentations | Given a topic, participants will present to the group, acknowledging the challenges of making effective presentations. | Have each participant take a few minutes to create a presentation on one of three topics: "Career goals," "Favorite hobby," or "What is your dream job?" Present to the group. | Flipchart |
| "The Good and the Bad" | Participants will gain an understanding of the features of a good presentation. | Participants break into groups to compile a list of what makes a good speech and a bad speech. Each group will present their findings. Instructor shows a video of a good speech. | PowerPoint slide titled "The Good, the Bad, and the Ugly," video equipment |
| "Pizzazz" | Participants will learn tactics for engaging audience attention. | Lecturette: Instructor leads a discussion on what "pizzazz" looks like in a presentation and how to utilize it properly. | Handout on different forms of "pizzazz." |
| Break | | | |
| Get organized, get comfortable, get positive | Participants will learn how to structure their presentations, presentation dos and don'ts, and how to overcome fear. | Lecturette: Discuss mind mapping and three buckets. Exercise: "Power of Positive." | PowerPoint slide on organization, flipchart |

| | | | |
|---|---|---|---|
| Assignment and prepare for presentations | Participants will use their new skills to prepare a one-minute presentation. | Participants will receive their topics for presenting. The instructor will give details on videotaping. | PowerPoint presentation explaining assignment |
| Lights, camera, action! | Participants will present in front of the audience and video camera utilizing their presentation delivery skills. | Participant deliver presentations (filmed, with verbal or written feedback). | Video camera |
| Wrap-up | Participants will review key content points during a group discussion. | Solicit from the group what new information they will take away from the session. Write them on a flipchart. | Flipchart |
| Video takeaway | Participants will take away a video recording of their presentation. | Explain the importance of filming yourself. | Video recordings |

## Table 7-2. Matrix of Instructor Styles, Strategies, and Activities in the "Delivering Effective Presentations" Workshop

| Topic | Style | Strategy | Tactic |
|---|---|---|---|
| Instructor Introduction | Systematic Safe Stimulating | 3. Set clear and meaningful objectives. <br> 16. Help participants feel at home. <br> 17. Let participants know what to expect. <br> 19. Keep time commitments. <br> 20. Build trust and openness. <br> 6. Present info in interesting, useful ways. | 3.1 <br> 16.1, 16.3, 16.4, 16.6 <br> 17.1, 17.2 <br> 19.5 <br> 20.7 <br> 6.3 |
| 30-Second Presentations | Spontaneous Stimulating | 14. Build in risk taking. <br> 8. Encourage creativity. | 14.1 <br> 8.4, 8.3 |

| "The Good and the Bad" | Stimulating | 7. Use active learning approaches. | 7.6 |
| | | 6. Present info in interesting, useful ways. | 6.5 |
| | | 8. Encourage creativity. | 8.3 |
| "Pizzazz" | Stimulating | 6. Present info in interesting, useful ways. | 6.1, 6.4 |
| Break | | | |
| Get organized, get comfortable, get positive | Stimulating Safe | 6. Present info in interesting, useful ways. | 6.3, 6.4, 6.5 |
| | | 7. Use active learning approaches. | 7.1 |
| | | 20. Build trust and openness. | 20.7 |
| Assignment and preparation | Safe Stimulating | 17. Let participants know what to expect. | 17.1 |
| | | 10. Help participants practice new learning. | 10.2 |
| | | 8. Encourage creativity. | 8.2, 8.3 |
| Lights, camera, action! | Spontaneous Stimulating | 14. Build in risk taking. | 14.3 |
| | | 10. Help participants practice new learning. | 10.3, 10.7 |
| Wrap-up and evaluation | Systematic Spontaneous | 5. Evaluate your plan. | 5.9 |
| | | 15. Take time to reflect. | 15.7 |
| Video presentation | Stimulating | 10. Help participants practice new learning. | 10.3 |

## Plan the Workshop

This workshop topic is relevant to anyone who would like to gain presentation skills. The instructor will most likely not have any other information about the class participants and collaboration with them will have to occur during the session. If this is the case, utilize Tactic 1.3, "On-the-Spot Collaboration" and 1.5, "On-the-Spot Interviews" (systematic/ *Collaborate With Learners as You Plan*; see chapter 2). This can be slotted in during the "Instructor Introduction" module at the beginning of the workshop and the instructor can make changes to the program according to these findings.

If there is time to prepare the workshop to fit the specific needs of the participants, you can combine the strategies of *Collaborate With Learners as You Plan* and *Assess Learning Needs and Styles*. As chapter 2 explains, adults learn more effectively when they are included in the planning. Tactics such as 1.2, "Representative Group," and 1.4, "Interviews With Managers" both work well to involve the participants. Other tactics that are helpful in assessing learner needs are 2.6, "Informal Discussions" and 2.7, "Listing and Voting."

## Prepare the Room

The instructor should get to the workshop site at least an hour early to assess the learning environment. Though the room set-up may not take long, unforeseen problems often crop up. Be ready for anything: the room has been double-booked, the projector is not there, the chairs are down the hall, or the only key to the room is with the janitor who is home sick. Refer to Tactic 16.1, "Early Planning" (from the *Help Participants Feel at Home* strategy; see chapter 5). Prepare the equipment you know you'll be using in class. A room set up as a learning environment can include laptop and projector, a table set up with the latest books on presentation skills and public speaking, coffee and snacks, and a music player to create a comforting atmosphere. Depending on how many participants are enrolled in the program, the best seating arrangement for this type of workshop is the U-shape table arrangement. Getting to know each other and creating a safe environment are key elements in this class. It is too difficult to get to know someone who is sitting behind you. In such a workshop, where participants will be practicing their new skills in front of each other and giving and receiving feedback, it is imperative to use strategies from the safe instructor style. Refer to Tactics 16.3, "Welcoming Environment," 16.4, "Displays," and 16.6, "Add Your Special Touch" (from the *Help Participants Feel at Home* strategy; see chapter 5).

You will want to post the goals and agenda, including the instructional methods you plan to use. To inform participants of what to expect during the session, use Tactics 17.1, "Share Basic Instructional Information" and 19.5, "Publish the Agenda" (from the *Let Participants Know What to Expect* strategy; see chapter 5).

## Facilitate the Workshop

**Introduction and overview of class.** Let the participants know who you are! Adults need to know that the person standing up in front of them knows what she is talking about. Explain why you are qualified to teach them. Refer to Tactic 20.7, "Model Openness and Trust" (from the safe strategy *Build Trust and Openness*). Next, review the agenda, objectives, and exactly what is expected of participants. Explain that it is normal for anxiety to attend public speaking. Tie this in with the importance of organizing presentation information, using specific techniques to hold audience attention, and gaining self-awareness—all of which you will cover in the workshop.

## "Delivering Effective Presentations" Workshop Agenda

**Objectives**

Participants will:

- Identify the elements of a good presentation.
- Learn tactics for engaging an audience's attention.
- Understand how to organize presentation content by mind mapping and using three "content buckets."
- Become aware of the effect of body language, voice, and positive thinking on presentations.
- Record themselves giving one-minute presentations for take-home review.

**Methods**

- Lecturettes
- Skills application (in the form of participant presentations)
- Group discussions
- Handouts
- Exercises

**Agenda**

- Introduction and overview of class
- 30-second presentations
- What is a good presentation?
- "Pizzazz" and capturing audience attention
- Organization, comfort, and positive thinking
- Prepare participant presentations
- Present!
- Wrap up

**30-second presentations.** Explain that each participant will pick one of three topics that are displayed on the flipchart ("What are your career goals?" "What is your favorite hobby?" "What is your dream job?") and present a 30-second speech on their chosen topic. Give them a couple of minutes to think about what they want to say. They can use notes if they would like. Then have them present. See Tactics 14.1, "Meet New People" (from the spontaneous strategy *Build in Risk Taking*), and 8.4, "Set Clear Boundaries" (from the stimulating strategy, *Encourage Creativity*).

**What is a good presentation?** For a bit of humor and visual interest, refer to the film "The Good, the Bad, and the Ugly" starring Clint Eastwood by using it as the title of this module. You can use a clip or photo from the movie if you like. Refer to Tactic 6.3, "Visual Aids" (from the stimulating strategy, *Present Information in Interesting, Useful Ways*). Now that you have their attention, have the participants break out into groups of three and compile a list of what they think are the elements of a bad presentation and what they think are good. Have each group present their answers and the instructor will record them on a flipchart. Refer to Tactic 7.6, "Small Groups and Intergroup Sharing" (from the stimulating strategy *Use Active Learning Approaches*) and 14.5, "Perform Before Others" (from *Build in Risk Taking*). End with showing the group a short video example of a good speech.

**"Pizzazz."** Using Tactic 6.1, "The Lecturette" (from *Present Information in Interesting, Useful Ways*), explain the importance of adding interest to the presentation every six minutes to keep the audience's attention. As the instructor, be an example during your own presentation and add interest by using humor, self-disclosure stories, and so forth. Use the handout in Table 7-3 to help participants learn the different ways to keep an audience engaged. See Tactic 6.4, "Readings" (from *Present Information in Interesting, Useful Ways*).

## Table 7-3. Pizzazz: How to Dazzle Your Audience!

| Method | Description |
| --- | --- |
| Self-Disclosure | The presenter "discloses" an embarrassing moment or a mistake made. Participants like it when they know you are not perfect. |
| Common Ground | Find specific ways to relate to the audience. What do you have in common? |
| Stories/Examples | This is a great way to keep their attention, as long as they aren't too long or tangential. |
| Humor | Be very careful about jokes. And if stand-up comedy is not your thing, go light on this. But if you are good at it, this will give your participants a nice break from the training material. |

| Audience Involvement | Get them invested in the learning outcomes. Telling their own stories, responding to questions, and teaching part of the class are all ways to involve the audience and enhance their learning. |
|---|---|
| Demonstration | Many participants learn mainly by observation. An interesting demonstration will stimulate their learning. |
| Quotation | Quotes add emphasis to the points you make. They are also a great way to introduce and summarize content. |
| Name-Dropping | This can spark excitement whether the person is popular or not. "I heard Michele Bachmann say the other day..." or "Remember how George Costanza and Elaine would...?" |
| Props | Be creative in finding props that both grab the audience's attention and support the training content. |

**Get organized, get comfortable, get positive.** Conduct a discussion on organizing the presentation. See Tactic 6.5, "Demonstrations" (from *Present Information in Interesting, Useful Ways*). Lead the group in a mind-mapping exercise, which actively involves the participants in learning. Using Tactic 6.3, "Visual Aids" (from *Present Information in Interesting, Useful Ways*) write on a flipchart words or expressions that correlate with one another in each category. Explain that grouping like information in three categories keeps the presentation easy for the audience to follow. Now treat all of this information as if you are going to write an essay. Find a main point, or thesis. Create an introduction and conclusion that will grab audience attention and reinforce key points. Put it all together and you have an organized presentation.

Now that the participants know how to structure a presentation, show them how to deliver it with comfort. You might design a handout that helps speakers remember a few things to concentrate on while delivering a speech or presentation. Use Tactic 6.4, "Readings" (from *Present Information in Interesting, Useful Ways*) and have participants discuss the handout. You can also use a stimulating exercise (see Tactic 7.1, "Movement" from the strategy *Use Active Learning Approaches*). Have participants pair up. One will hold their arm up at shoulder height. The other partner will try pushing the arm down, while the person holding theirs up is trying to keep it up. Have that participant repeat "No, no, no." Watch how the arm comes down easily. Repeat this again but have the participant say

"Yes, yes, yes," while holding their arm up. Notice how it stays up! Now have them switch. Conclude with discussing the power of positive thinking on their presentation.

**Assignment and preparation.** See Tactic 17.1, "Share Basic Instructional Information" (from the safe strategy, *Let Participants Know What to Expect*). Assign each learner a topic for which they will deliver a presentation to the class. The objective of the exercise is to practice what they have learned about designing and delivering an effective presentation. Let them know that they will be filmed and that they will receive a copy of it at the end of the class. The purpose of the film is to observe their own performance and identify areas for improvement. See Tactic 10.2, "Demonstrate Using Skill Standards" (from the stimulating strategy *Help Participants Practice New Learning*). Giving the participants clear instructions, objectives, and a topic enables them to create a presentation in a short amount of time. See Tactic 8.2, "Provide Tools for Creativity" and 8.3, "Provide a Clear Example" (from the stimulating strategy *Encourage Creativity*).

**Lights, Camera, Action!** Have each participant deliver their presentation while you are filming. See Tactic 14.3, "Try New Skills" (from *Build in Risk Taking*), Tactic 10.3, "Video Feedback" (from *Help Participants Practice New Learning*) and Tactic 5.2, "Live Demonstrations" (from the systematic strategy *Evaluate Your Plan*).

**Wrap-up.** Take a few moments now to ask the participants what they have gained from the workshop. See Tactic 2.3, "Inquiry" (from the systematic strategy *Assess Participant Learning Needs and Styles*). Inform participants that there will always be opportunities for improvement if they continue to practice their skills and build on what they learned today.

**Video takeaway.** As mentioned earlier, Tactic 10.3, "Video Feedback" (from *Help Participants Practice New Learning*) will help participants identify their opportunities for improvements.

**Evaluation.** Provide copies of the evaluation form (Worksheet 7-1) either early on in the workshop or at the end of the day, and invite all to complete the form. After tabulating the ratings and reading over the comments, the instructor can modify and improve the workshop (from *Evaluate Your Plan*; see the discussion of questionnaires on page 30).

## Worksheet 7-1. Workshop Evaluation Form: "Delivering Effective Presentations"

*Rate to what extent the workshop has met each of the learning objectives below. (1 = little, 2 = some, 3 = much, 4 = very much)*

| | | | | | |
|---|---|---|---|---|---|
| 1. | Identify the elements of a good presentation. | 1 | 2 | 3 | 4 |
| 2. | List methods of adding interest to a presentation. | 1 | 2 | 3 | 4 |
| 3. | Understand how to organize a presentation. | 1 | 2 | 3 | 4 |
| 4. | Become aware of body language, voice, and positive thinking in presentations. | 1 | 2 | 3 | 4 |

List some things that you liked about this workshop:

_____

_____

_____

List some things that might be improved:

_____

_____

_____

Your message to the instructor:

_____

_____

_____

_____

_____

_____

_____

_____

# 8. Plan Your Continual Improvement

We are creatures of habit—necessarily so because the routines and patterns we form provide us the freedom to concentrate on the unpredictable aspects of our lives. We put much of our lives on autopilot, a tactic that helps us survive an endlessly changing world. Our need to create patterns of thinking and behaving has a downside, however. When we are called upon to be creative, respond to unique situations, or learn new behaviors, these rigid patterns may hinder us from adapting or developing unique and creative responses.

How do we break out of our molds to meet unique problems or changing circumstances? We are able to change and adapt when we are forced to do so. We also alter our set ways when we are self-aware; willing to assess our beliefs and behaviors and see the need for improvement or change. Such awareness requires self-esteem, self-actualization, confidence, belief in one's ultimate worth, and being "centered."

As an instructor, you may find that you have some well-worn ways of teaching. These ways may suit you just fine, but to be more effective you may need to explore other ways as well. If you are reading this section on continual improvement, you must be having some thoughts about how to be a better teacher. If you have read the previous chapters, you know that a balanced approach (equally applying all four of the instructor styles) is best when teaching adults. If you strive for that balance, you will find it leads you on a path to continual improvement. To make progress you must become aware of how you teach, make a commitment to achieve balance, and try out new instructional strategies and learning activities. We are not talking about a complete makeover, but simply adding to your repertoire of strategies and tactics.

## Accepting and Acting on Helpful Criticism

In the children's story, "The Emperor's New Clothes," an emperor imagines he has wonderful new clothes but is, in fact, completely naked. No one, except an innocent child, dared tell him the truth. Avoiding criticism is one sure way to get mired in rigidity, but it is quite a normal behavior. We tend not to notice painful truths about ourselves. It may be especially difficult to accept critical remarks as an instructor—you are, after all, an expert on your topic!

The aim of *Teach With Style* is to challenge instructors to make continual improvements. That means accepting critical feedback on your work and changing accordingly. Of course, there are many ways to teach. It is important that you align your unique personality and natural strengths to the role of the teacher. Strike a balance between pushing yourself to change and appreciating yourself as you are.

When you get feedback from a group of participants, you may be tempted to retain the good comments and high marks and discount the criticism. Or, perhaps you dwell on the few negative comments and shrug off praise. This is also counterproductive. Naturally, a balanced approach is best. Celebrate your strengths as reflected in positive feedback from your participants, but remain receptive to criticism. Helpful criticism is solicited and points out specific errors rather than taking the form of a general rebuke. ("What a boring class.") Taking a critical look at yourself is never easy. If you are resistant to constructive criticism based on accurate feedback, you will not achieve continual improvement. Step back and see what you could do to make realistic changes.

## Inventories as Tools for Continual Improvement

This chapter offers a process and tools for continual improvement. The following steps will help you improve continually as you teach.

1.  Begin by learning your *instructor style* by using the *"What's My Style?" Words List Inventory*. After completing this inventory you are ready to get feedback from your students and a third-party observer.

2.  Use the *Self-Assessment Inventory* to assess what strategies you should strengthen or use more often.

3.  Use the *Participant Inventories* to assess how participants experience your instruction.

4.  Invite an observer to use the *Observer Inventory* for further analysis.

5.  Finally, you are ready to plan your improvement by using the *Instructor Improvement Worksheet* and the A.I.M. process.

This process becomes a "cycle of improvement" when it is used repeatedly in your efforts to become a better teacher. (See Figure 8-1.)

**Figure 8-1. The Continual Improvement Cycle**

## Instructor Assessment Inventories

You are encouraged to use the inventories in this section often, particularly the participant inventories. These tools will guide your continual improvement. Getting critical responses that represent different points of view is very helpful. How do you, as the teacher, perceive your styles and strategies? How do your participants experience your instruction? How does an objective observer assess your work? You get a well-rounded and accurate picture from combining these three perspectives. Pay attention to patterns in the feedback you receive: Do they reveal a tendency to employ certain strategies and tactics more than others?

## Table 8-1. What's My Style? Words List Inventory

*Select the list of words that best describes you and the one that least describes you.*

| SAFE | STIMULATING | SPONTANEOUS | SYSTEMATIC |
|------|-------------|-------------|------------|
| I AM... | I AM... | I AM... | I AM... |
| ☐ Caring | ☐ Challenging | ☐ Playful | ☐ Purposeful |
| ☐ Sympathetic | ☐ Charismatic | ☐ Enthusiastic | ☐ Realistic |
| ☐ Sensitive | ☐ Intuitive | ☐ Interactive | ☐ Analytical |
| ☐ A Good Listener | ☐ Stimulating | ☐ Funny | ☐ Thorough |
| ☐ A Peacemaker | ☐ Dynamic Leader | ☐ A Storyteller | ☐ A Planner |
| ☐ A Servant Of Others | ☐ A Confronter | ☐ Gregarious | ☐ A Researcher |
| ☐ A Comforter | ☐ Willing To Lead | ☐ Action-Oriented | ☐ A Rule-Keeper |
| ☐ Accepting of All | ☐ Principled | ☐ Childlike | ☐ Logical |
| ☐ Soothing | ☐ Persuasive | ☐ Engaging | ☐ Effective |
| ☐ Tender-Hearted | ☐ A Motivating Speaker | ☐ Creative | ☐ An Evaluator |
| ☐ Good Host/ Hostess | ☐ Confident | ☐ Lively | ☐ Goal-Oriented |
| ☐ Approachable | ☐ Immovable | ☐ Emotive | ☐ Accountable |
| | | ☐ Inventive | ☐ Organized |
| ☐ This Is Mostly Me | ☐ This Is Mostly Me | ☐ This Is Mostly Me | ☐ This Is Mostly Me |
| ☐ This Is Somewhat Me | ☐ This Is Somewhat Me | ☐ This Is Somewhat Me | ☐ This Is Somewhat Me |
| ☐ This Is Not Me | ☐ This Is Not Me | ☐ This Is Not Me | ☐ This Is Not Me |

## Table 8-2. What's My Style? Instructor Profiles

| | Safe | Stimulating | Spontaneous | Systematic |
|---|---|---|---|---|
| **Instructor style** | This instructor uses group-building exercises and ensures that learners feel welcomed and comfortable. | This instructor uses active learning approaches and stresses change and growth in the learner. | This instructor uses fun and creative activities to make the learning enjoyable and surprising. | This instructor uses clear objectives to design and deliver well-targeted, organized training. |
| **Students' experience** | The learning atmosphere is very welcoming and comfortable. Students know they are accepted and respected. | The learning challenges and provokes change and growth. Students find they learn many valuable things they can use. | The learning is enjoyable and full of surprise and laughter. Students have a good time and feel happy. | The learning experience is well-structured and organized. Students know exactly what will happen and how they will benefit. |
| **Goal of instruction** | Friendly learning atmosphere conducive to learning | Effective change | Enjoyment and freedom | Meet learning objectives |
| **Key words** | Acceptance Comfort Getting acquainted | Change Challenge Provocative | Enjoyment Unpredictable Humorous | Order Objectives Well-planned |
| **Advantages for learners** | They don't have to worry about being embarrassed or uncomfortable. Learners find a friendly place where they can relax and learn. | They don't have to put up with "talking heads" or death-by-slideshows. Learners find they are challenged to think, feel, and act in new ways. | They don't have to worry about spending time in boring sessions. Learners find that time passes quickly and they feel refreshed and happy. | They don't have to worry about a mismatch between what they want and what they get. Learners find the experience meets their real needs. |
| **What this instructor needs to learn** | This instructor could learn from the stimulating style to challenge learners to change and grow. | This instructor could learn from the safe style to ensure the acceptance and comfort of learners. | This instructor could learn from the systematic style to incorporate more order and predictability in training. | This instructor could learn from the spontaneous style to provide more freedom and enjoyment in training. |

## Worksheet 8-1. Instructor Self-Assessment Inventory

Name:                                              Date:

After you thoroughly review the instructor styles and strategies in this book, rate how often you use the strategies listed below.

Key:
1 = Never use this strategy            4 = Frequently use this strategy
2 = Seldom use this strategy           5 = Always use this strategy
3 = Sometimes use this strategy        NA = Not applicable in my teaching

**Make It Systematic:**
___Collaborate with your learners as you plan.
___Assess participant learning needs and styles.
___Set clear, meaningful goals.
___Plan to reach your goals.
___Evaluate your plan.

**Make It Stimulating:**
___Present information in interesting and useful ways.
___Use active learning approaches.
___Encourage creativity.
___Help participants solve real problems.
___Help participants practice new learning.

**Make It Spontaneous:**
___Help participants tell their stories.
___Make it funny, make it fun.
___Use imagination and the arts.
___Build in risk taking.
___Take time to reflect.

**Make It Safe:**
___Help participants feel at home.
___Let participants know what to expect.
___Help participants get acquainted.
___Keep time commitments.
___Build trust and openness.

Go back over the strategies and mark the ones you want to begin improving and using more.

## Worksheet 8-2. Participant Inventory: Instructor Styles

Session Title:                                                        Date:

Name of Instructor(s):

Help the instructor(s) make improvements by completing this form. Rate to what extent the four conditions (safe, stimulating, systematic, and spontaneous) were present in this session.

Please circle the number that best fits:

| The instruction was… | NONE | | SOME | | | MUCH |
|---|---|---|---|---|---|---|
| Safe: I felt relaxed, comfortable, and able to interact with other participants. | 0 | 1 | 2 | 3 | 4 | 5 |
| Stimulating: I was actively challenged to learn new ideas and skills. | 0 | 1 | 2 | 3 | 4 | 5 |
| Systematic: A clear, logical teaching plan was explained and followed. | 0 | 1 | 2 | 3 | 4 | 5 |
| Spontaneous: There was a free-flow of ideas, humor, and fun. | 0 | 1 | 2 | 3 | 4 | 5 |

What did you like best about this instruction?

_____

_____

Suggestions to improve the instruction:

_____

_____

Other comments for the instructor(s):

_____

_____

## Worksheet 8-3. Participant Inventory: Instructor Strategies

Session Title:                                                    Date:

Name of Instructor(s):

Instructions: The purpose of this assessment is to help the instructor(s) improve. You will evaluate the strategies used by the instructor(s). Circle the number that best represents your opinion of the instruction you received. 1 = little, 3 = some, 5 = much.

**Safe**

| | | | | | | |
|---|---|---|---|---|---|---|
| 1. | The learning space was comfortable. | 1 | 2 | 3 | 4 | 5 |
| 2. | We were well aware of what to expect. | 1 | 2 | 3 | 4 | 5 |
| 3. | We had time to warm up and get acquainted. | 1 | 2 | 3 | 4 | 5 |
| 4. | The instructor kept to the agreed-upon schedule. | 1 | 2 | 3 | 4 | 5 |
| 5. | Learning tasks enabled us to interact freely. | 1 | 2 | 3 | 4 | 5 |

**Stimulating**

| | | | | | | |
|---|---|---|---|---|---|---|
| 6. | I was challenged to learn and apply new ideas. | 1 | 2 | 3 | 4 | 5 |
| 7. | We were actively engaged in learning. | 1 | 2 | 3 | 4 | 5 |
| 8. | We were encouraged to be creative. | 1 | 2 | 3 | 4 | 5 |
| 9. | We solved real and important problems we face. | 1 | 2 | 3 | 4 | 5 |
| 10. | We practiced new skills. | 1 | 2 | 3 | 4 | 5 |

**Systematic**

| | | | | | | |
|---|---|---|---|---|---|---|
| 11. | The participants helped plan the instruction. | 1 | 2 | 3 | 4 | 5 |
| 12. | Instruction was based on our needs and learning styles. | 1 | 2 | 3 | 4 | 5 |
| 13. | The objectives of the class were clear and made sense. | 1 | 2 | 3 | 4 | 5 |
| 14. | I felt that I learned what I needed and wanted. | 1 | 2 | 3 | 4 | 5 |
| 15. | Participants evaluated the instruction. | 1 | 2 | 3 | 4 | 5 |

**Spontaneous**

| | | | | | |
|---|---|---|---|---|---|
| 16. We worked together in small groups. | 1 | 2 | 3 | 4 | 5 |
| 17. We enjoyed ourselves, laughed, and had fun. | 1 | 2 | 3 | 4 | 5 |
| 18. We used our imaginations or artistic expression. | 1 | 2 | 3 | 4 | 5 |
| 19. The instructor helped us take risks to learn. | 1 | 2 | 3 | 4 | 5 |
| 20. There was time for thoughtful reflection. | 1 | 2 | 3 | 4 | 5 |

## Worksheet 8-4. Observer Inventory

Session Title:                                                    Date and Location:

Name of Instructor(s):                                    Observer:

**How to use this inventory:**
1. The Observer Inventory is to be used by "invitation only." Choose someone whom you trust to be objective. One of your participants can fill this role if you feel he is capable.
2. The observer rates the extent to which you use each of the instructor strategies using this scale: 1 = little, 3 = some, 5 = much, or N/A = not applicable.
3. The observer notes the actual behavior observed that demonstrates the strategy.
4. The observer can make comments about your use or lack of use of the strategies.
5. The observer and the instructor spend some time going over the inventory after the instruction is complete.

**Make It Safe**
1. The learning space helped participants feel relaxed and welcome.
   Rating:
   Evidence:
   Comments:

2. Participants were able to discuss and negotiate the objectives, methods, schedule, and content.
   Rating:
   Evidence:
   Comments:

3. There was time to warm up so adults could get to know each other and the instructor, and to develop an interest in the topic.
Rating:
Evidence:
Comments:

4. The instructor kept to the schedule as agreed upon.
Rating:
Evidence:
Comments:

5. Participants had a sense of closeness with others and were able to share concerns and help others solve problems.
Rating:
Evidence:
Comments:

Total Safe Rating:

**Make It Stimulating**
6. The participants were challenged with interesting, new, and useful information.
Rating:
Evidence:
Comments:

7. The participants were involved in active learning tasks at least 50 percent of the time.
Rating:
Evidence:
Comments:

8. Participants were able to develop and practice new skills and behaviors.
Rating:
Evidence:
Comments:

9. The participants were engaged in solving real and important problems that they face.
Rating:
Evidence:
Comments:

10. Participants received feedback on their progress.
    Rating:
    Evidence:
    Comments:

Total Stimulating Rating:

**Make It Systematic**

11. The instruction was well targeted and flexible in meeting participant needs.
    Rating:
    Evidence:
    Comments:

12. The instruction was based on participant needs and learning preferences.
    Rating:
    Evidence:
    Comments:

13. Participants were accurately informed about learning goals, objectives, and methods.
    Rating:
    Evidence:
    Comments:

14. Participants indicated that they learned what they needed and wanted.
    Rating:
    Evidence:
    Comments:

15. Participants received information about the overall effectiveness of the program.
    Rating:
    Evidence:
    Comments:

Total Systematic Rating:

**Make It Spontaneous**

16. Participants learned by sharing their knowledge and experience.
    Rating:
    Evidence:
    Comments:

17. The training incorporated playfulness; participants laughed and
    enjoyed themselves.
    Rating:
    Evidence:
    Comments:

18. Participants engaged in creative expression as a way of enhancing their learning.
    Rating:
    Evidence:
    Comments:

19. The instructor promoted risk taking and modeled willingness to change.
    Rating:
    Evidence:
    Comments:

20. Time was made for silence, quiet reflection, and journaling to integrate new ideas.
    Rating:
    Evidence:
    Comments:

Total Spontaneous Rating:

## A.I.M. for Improvement

A simple way to plan for continual improvement is to use the A.I.M. problem-solving method:

A = Actual, or how I am doing right now.

I = Ideal, or how I want to be doing in the future.

M = Method, or how I will get from the Actual to the Ideal.

In addition, you will need to determine the outcome of your plan. It is important to follow each step in sequence. Two common errors made in problem solving include selecting a solution before the problem is clarified and the goal is defined, and jumping from the problem clarification to a solution. Following this process is essential for the best results.

## Figure 8-2. The AIM Problem-Solving Method
AIM for Continual Instructor Improvement

**A** = ACTUAL
PERFORMANCE
Diagnose your
current performance.

*My performance gap*

**I** = IDEAL PERFORMANCE
Determine your
desired performance.

**O** = OUTCOME
Determine if the
performance gap
is closed.

**M** = METHOD
Determine how you will
improve your performance.

## A = Actual

The first step is to examine how you are actually doing right now. What are your strengths and weaknesses? If you have already identified some areas for improvement, focus on these. Refer to the instructor feedback inventories provided in this chapter to make one or more diagnostic statements concerning your needs for improvement. For example: "I have been planning my sessions without adequately assessing the needs and interests of my participants."

## I = Ideal

Consider how you want your instruction to improve. Use your *Actual* statements as a guide for setting your goals. Be specific about what you want. Make it your goal to strengthen the styles and strategies you use less often. Write one or more goal statements. For example: "I want to incorporate more creative learning tactics in my training programs."

## M = Method

The final step is to select methods that will get you from the *Actual* to the *Ideal*. Use the *Ideal* statements to create your plan for improvement. Make one or more statements that will describe your plan. For example: "I will consult several training and adult education books and articles and find 10 good ways to assess participant needs and interests. I will use the best methods consistently over the next six months."

## Outcome

Finally, you will also want to add specific target dates by which you will make these changes. Pinning down the date by which you will accomplish your goal is a powerful motivator. It helps to have at least one other person to hold you accountable. Decide how you will determine when the gap between *Actual* and *Ideal* has closed. The participant and observer inventories provided in this chapter are helpful for determining whether you have achieved your goals.

Use Worksheet 8-5 to guide you through the A.I.M. process.

### Worksheet 8-5. Instructor Continual Improvement Worksheet

**A = Actual**

1. What did you discover about your instructor style from the *"What's My Style?" Words List*? What is your dominant style?

2. What is the result from the *Instructor Self-Assessment*?

3. What is the result from the *Participant Inventory: Instructor Styles*?

4. What is the result from the *Participant Inventory: Instructor Strategies*?

5. What is the result from the *Observer Inventory*?

Diagnose your current performance and areas for improvement. Make diagnostic statements for each area of need.

_____

_____

**I = Ideal**

Set goals for improvement: Make parallel statements to the *Actual* statements above that describe how you want your instruction to be improved. Which of these *Ideal* statements are most important to you right now?

_____

_____

**M = Method**

Plan to improve: Describe in specific terms what you will do to accomplish the ideal.

_____

_____

**Plan for Outcomes**

Deliver results: Decide when you will accomplish your goals for improvement and how you will determine that your goals have been met.

_____

_____

# 12 Ideas for Self-Development

The following ideas will get you thinking about your plans for continual improvement as an instructor.

1. Resource Lists. Develop a list of books, journals, and other sources that you can study to develop each strategy. Create a resource file or notebook with new ideas.

2. Support Group. Meet with other instructors and develop a small support group to work toward improvement.

3. Attend Training. There are many organizations that offer "train-the-trainer" programs. Do some research to find those that best fit your needs.

4. Self-Directed Development. Conduct your own specific needs assessment; create specific objectives; plan to learn and apply your learning; and evaluate your learning.

5. Consult an Expert. Do you know someone who has much skill and experience in the strategy you want to develop? Seek out that person for consultation, mentoring, or coaching.

6. Multimedia Presentations. Watch or listen to audio or video presentations on your topic of choice.

7. Brainstorm and Create. Sit down with others or go on a personal mini-retreat to develop new learning tactics that support the instructor strategies you most want to focus on.

8. Buddy System. Find a colleague who has similar development goals and form a pact to learn together and support each other.

9. Consult Your Participants. You can gain valuable insight into your strengths and weaknesses as an instructor from your participants. Make a special effort to encourage thorough and honest feedback from your participants. Ask them many questions and listen carefully to their answers.

10. Join a Professional Association. Professional associations are usually focused on improving their members' knowledge and skills. You can take advantage of their many resources, including publications, conferences, and networking opportunities.

11. Online Learning. Sign up for webinars or other online learning resources. Use Facebook, LinkedIn, Twitter, or other social media platforms to network with colleagues, participate in discussions related to your profession, and access information about your industry.

12. Websites. Regularly visit websites that offer information about your profession and topic of expertise.

## Summary

The continual improvement process, instructor inventories, and the planning worksheet provide you ways to gain insight into your weaknesses and strengths as an instructor. These tools are provided as a means for improving your instruction but the time and effort you put into it will determine your success. If you use these tools conscientiously, you will improve significantly as an instructor, and your participants will benefit as learners.

The Teach With Style model offers all the elements you need to become a confident, competent instructor. The styles, strategies, and learning activities, as well as sample workshops, provide a hands-on guide to help you design and implement balanced, effective instruction. Tools for continual improvement guarantee your ongoing effectiveness in teaching adults.

# Recommended Reading

Barbazette, Jean. (2006). *The Art of Great Training Delivery: Strategies, Tools, and Tactics.* San Francisco, CA: Pfeiffer.
This is a detailed, analytical approach to training written with both new and experienced trainers in mind—a nice resource that covers the basics.

Bergen, Sharon. (2009). *Best Practices for Training Early Childhood Professionals.* St. Paul, MN: Redleaf Press.
The title tells it all. Use this as a beginner's guide to the basics of training in the early childhood education field.

Biech, Elaine. (2009). *10 Steps to Successful Training.* Alexandria, VA: ASTD Press.
This book is described by Mel Silberman as a "clearly written, user-friendly book" to enable any trainer. It's designed mainly for new trainers. Start here.

Biech, Elaine, ed. (2007). *90 World-Class Activities by 90 World-Class Trainers.* San Francisco, CA: Pfeiffer.
Trainers from all over the world each share their favorite learning activity. Top-notch ideas that get your trainer blood pumping—trust us!

Broad, M.L., and J.W. Newstrom. (1992). *Transfer of Training: Action-Packed Strategies to Ensure High Payoff From Training Investments.* Perseus Publishing.
The problem of learning retention and transfer is often overlooked. This book presents a systematic process for training transfer.

Dirksen, Julie. (2012). *Design for How People Learn*. Berkeley, CA: New Riders.
Dirksen gets to the heart of the current science of adult learning fundamentals. This book shows you how to attract and maintain your audience's attention and make learning stick!

Hayes, Elisabeth R., and Arthur L. Wilson, eds. (2000). *Handbook of Adult and Continuing Education*. San Francisco, CA: Jossey-Bass.
This rich handbook gives you a solid foundation as a trainer, as it reflects on the body of science that helps build effective training principles and strategies for different settings and participants.

Holton, Elwood F., and Richard A. Swanson. (2011). *The Adult Learner*, 5th edition. Burlington, MA: Butterworth-Heinemann.
This is the "bible" of adult education, helping the profession understand andragogy and how adults need to be in charge of their learning.

Jones, Elizabeth. (2007). *Teaching Adults Revisited: Active Learning for Early Childhood Educators*. NAEYC.
A classic that follows this master educator as she teaches the introductory course in Educational Credential Evaluators (ECE)!

Klatt, Bruce. (1999). *The Ultimate Training Workshop Handbook: A Comprehensive Guide to Leading Successful Workshops and Training Programs*. Boston, MA: McGraw Hill.
This is a terrific reference for any trainer's library. It presents a step-by-step guide, from meeting with the client and securing the stage to evaluating the results of the workshop or training session. 500+ pages of timeless information.

Lakey, George. (2010). *Facilitating Group Learning: Strategies for Success With Diverse Adult Learners*. San Francisco, CA: Jossey-Bass.
Lakey teaches what he calls "direct education"—which he says "cuts through the fluff and pretense that distances the learners from the subject." Shows how to effectively teach those on the margins of our society.

Mager, Roger F. (1997). *Preparing Instructional Objectives: A Critical Tool in the Development of Effective Instruction*, 3rd ed. Atlanta, GA: CEP Press.
Objectives create a roadmap for training. This is an easy read and well respected by many in the field.

Silberman, Mel. (2006). *Active Training: A Handbook of Techniques, Designs, Case Examples, and Tips*, 3rd ed. San Francisco, CA: Pfeiffer.

A must-have resource for any new or experienced trainer. There is everything from "brain-friendly lectures" to "controlling timing and pacing of training sessions" and much, much more. We would call it the standard—Mel Silberman is the Malcolm Knowles of modern training.

Silberman, Mel. (2005). *101 Ways to Make Training Active*, 2nd ed. San Francisco, CA: Pfeiffer.

Lots of tips and techniques that really work. Topics include stimulating discussions, peer teaching, on-the-spot assessments, and emotional intelligence. A smorgasbord of well-organized ideas!

Silberman, Mel. (2005). *Teaching Actively: Eight Steps and 32 Strategies to Spark Learning in Any Classroom*. Boston, MA: Pearson, Allyn & Bacon.

Feeling stale? This is the book for you! This book is a compendium of strategies and ideas to perk up your training delivery.

# About the Authors

**Jim Teeters** has been a family-life educator, college professor, staff development specialist, pastor, private workshop leader, and trainer of adult instructors. He has spent a year in China teaching English to university students and faculty. He has a bachelor's degree in sociology from the University of Washington and a master's degree in social work from the University of Hawaii. Jim published a book on teaching religious education to all ages (*Going Intergenerational: All Ages Learning Bible Truths Together*, 2010), is a published poet, and has written a novel with his grandson.

**Lynn Hodges** was first exposed to teaching adults while working as a flight attendant at Northwest Airlines. She became certified as a training specialist and went on to teach a variety of subjects, such as leadership, conflict management, and security response to terrorism in the airline industry. She later became a certified instructor for the Speakers Training Camp. Lynn has a bachelor's degree in interdisciplinary studies of social and behavioral sciences with a minor in communications. She currently teaches adults how to organize and deliver great speeches and presentations, in addition to her regular flight attendant duties.

# Index